# Think About It

Ezra Earl Jones

*Reflections on Quality and
The United Methodist Church*

Library of Congress Catalog Card No. 95-071338

ISBN 0-88177-148-1

Unless otherwise indicated, all scripture quotations are taken from the New Revised Standard Version of the Holy Bible.

Think About It: Reflections on Quality and The United Methodist Church. Copyright © 1996 Ezra Earl Jones. All rights reserved. Printed in the United States. No part of this book may be reproduced in any form whatsoever, print or electronic, without written permission from the publisher except in the case of brief quotations embodied in critical articles or reviews. For information contact Discipleship Resources Editorial Offices, P. O. Box 840, Nashville, TN 37202, (615) 340-7068.

DR148

CONTENTS

*Foreword by Bishop David Lawson* ..................................................................iv
*Introduction* ........................................................................................................vi

**Chapter 1: Current Reality in The United Methodist Church** ........................1
    Creeping Congregationalism in a Connectional System ...........................2
    Apportionments ...........................................................................................4
    A Room with No Windows ..........................................................................6
    Appointments ..............................................................................................8
    Impressions of the 1992 General Conference .........................................10
    The Doctor and the Church ......................................................................12
    Sometimes You Can See Only from the Inside ......................................14
    Organizations in Decline ..........................................................................15
    Bloated with Bureaucracy ........................................................................17
    Lofty Visions and Continued Decline .......................................................19
    Exclusive Territories .................................................................................22
    We Don't Need This .................................................................................24

**Chapter 2: Systems, the Primary Task of the Church,
and the People We Serve** ................................................................................27
    Getting New Results Requires a New System ........................................28
    Blaming .....................................................................................................30
    Improving the System ...............................................................................32
    Won't He Ever Learn! ...............................................................................34
    Primary Task .............................................................................................35
    Christian Community ................................................................................38
    More About Christian Community ...........................................................41
    Members and Customers ........................................................................43
    Evangelism ...............................................................................................46
    Wow! Was She Ever Wrong! ...................................................................48
    Marketing the Church ...............................................................................50
    Let's Not Turn the Message Into Bait ......................................................52
    Confusion About the Journey ...................................................................54
    A New Quest? Let's Focus on Essentials ...............................................57

**Chapter 3: Quality Improvement and Change** ..............................................61
    Quality Is Guaranteed ..............................................................................62
    The New and the Old ...............................................................................63
    When the Revolution Comes, Everything Changes ...............................65
    Building Knowledge .................................................................................68
    Satisfaction Guaranteed ..........................................................................70

Getting It Backward ..................................................................................72
A Bishop Responds to Concerns About Quality Improvement ..................73
Moments of Truth........................................................................................76
Always Another Call ...................................................................................78

**Chapter 4: Mission, Vision, and Leadership** ...............................................81
Leaders with a 100-Year Vision ..................................................................82
Denial...........................................................................................................84
Who Can Lead Us?......................................................................................86
Leadership...................................................................................................88
Leadership—One More Time......................................................................90
Listening to the Laity ..................................................................................92
Ordinary Times ...........................................................................................93
From Conversation to Improvement ..........................................................96
Social Witness ............................................................................................97
When the Vision Indicts the Present..........................................................99
"Guaranteed Appointment!" I'm For It!...................................................102

FOREWORD

# Let's "Defrag" the Church

Ezra Earl Jones seeks to help us "defrag" the church. In this series of writings, he repeatedly extends invitations to church leaders. He suggests that the church's potential for ministry ranges far beyond anything we are currently allowing. He suggests that there is a way to free the church from that which binds it, to overcome the church's fragmentation, and to focus its full potential on its mission.

Cynicism in the church frequently undercuts leadership. Dr. Jones, however, celebrates the way God's Spirit works among us, creating vision and hope. His are encouraging words.

Many of you who read this book are computer literate. You therefore know how scrambled the computer's memory can become as a document is altered and made larger. Recognizing that the space occupied by that file is not large enough, the computer will either move the whole file to another location or deposit the leftover portion in a new location. You delete a file, leaving an empty space on the disk. The open space is too large for the next file and thus another segment of space is left empty. After a time, the computer works much less efficiently because it must search for all the fragmented pieces before it can bring the completed file to the screen.

As computer users, we need the program called "Defrag." When the controls for that program appear on the screen, we see a command called "optimize." When we touch that control, the program will "defragment" the computer's memory, rejoin fragmented segments of each file, relocate some files, and thus optimize the effectiveness of the computer. The full capacity of the computer is then available for the work in process.

*Think About It* helps us understand the necessity of "defragmenting" the church as a way of optimizing our church systems. Dr. Jones helps us see how we can focus on our primary task, "defragment" our resources, and release our creativity into improved service of our Christian mission.

The one thing the computer's "Defrag" program will not do is tell us what our most important and highest priority should be. It simply optimizes the working of the computer to help us in our efforts. *We* must decide what purpose best defines who we are and what we are to do. Dr. Jones, in *Think About It*, seeks to help us examine our primary task as the church. In reflecting on the congregation, he writes: "The primary task of the Christian congregation is that weekly, repeatable cycle of reaching out to people who are burdened by persistent guilt and bringing them into the fellowship of the church, creating settings for them to experience the renewing power of God in their lives, nurturing them in the disciplines of Christian living, and then sending them out to live differently, as disciples of Christ who work for justice and love among all people."

However, Dr. Jones makes it clear that the identification of the church's primary task is finally our responsibility. His questions and suggestions intend to prod us to address the issue in new, systemic ways.

Ezra Earl Jones is appreciated as the general secretary of the General Board of Discipleship, a long-time church consultant, and a supportive friend of many in the church. Under his leadership, the General Board of Discipleship of The United Methodist Church has been engaged in a quest for an improved way to serve congregations. He and his staff have been asking, "How can this agency best resource the mission of the local congregation? How can a denominational board be sensitive to the needs and hopes of the congregations? How can the staff of the board best work together to respond to these needs with forward-leaning resources?"

The tools needed for reading this book include a notebook, pencil, and time for reflection. *Think About It* raises questions that will prompt further questions and beginning thoughts in the reader.

—BISHOP DAVID J. LAWSON
Bishop, Illinois Area
President of the General Board of Discipleship, 1992-1996

# Introduction

*Think About It* is a collection of articles written by Ezra Earl Jones, general secretary of the United Methodist General Board of Discipleship, over a period of five years.

Each article originally appeared as a *Perspective* article, a reflection piece inserted each month in the General Board of Discipleship's newsletter *Discipleship Dateline*. Begun in January 1991, *Perspective* is intended to raise issues and concerns of importance to United Methodist leaders. Each *Perspective* article ends with the words "Think About It"—a fitting title for a five-year collection of those articles.

Response to *Perspective* has been positive, and numerous calls for back issues prompted General Board of Discipleship staff to request the publication of a five-year anniversary collection. Because *Perspective* has a fairly limited audience, staff members wanted to offer the church at large an opportunity to encounter these thought-provoking pieces. Ezra Earl Jones consented to his colleagues' request, and *Think About It* was born.

Not all articles that appeared in *Perspective* over the period 1991-1995 are included. Some were time-bound and thus inappropriate for a general collection.

The articles have been grouped according to subject matter. The date of original publication appears at the end of each article.

We, the staff of the General Board of Discipleship, hope you enjoy this collection. Write to us and let us know what you "Think About It."

—CHERYL CAPSHAW
 Editor

# CHAPTER 1:

## CURRENT REALITY IN THE UNITED METHODIST CHURCH

Creeping Congregationalism in a Connectional System ...................... 2
Apportionments .................................................................................. 4
A Room with No Windows .................................................................. 6
Appointments ...................................................................................... 8
Impressions of the 1992 General Conference .................................. 10
The Doctor and the Church .............................................................. 12
Sometimes You Can See Only from the Inside ................................ 14
Organizations in Decline .................................................................. 15
Bloated with Bureaucracy ................................................................ 17
Lofty Visions and Continued Decline ................................................ 19
Exclusive Territories ........................................................................ 22
We Don't Need This .......................................................................... 24

# Creeping Congregationalism in a Connectional System

We've seen it before. The typist hits the wrong key, and the Sunday bulletin announces the morning worship for the "Wesley Memorial *Untied* Methodist Church."

While some people laugh at the error, others wonder if it hints of things to come. The typographical error has a ring of prophecy. "*Untied* Methodist Church" flashes the warning—like a blinking neon sign in the night.

We aren't "untied" yet, but we are unraveling around the edges as we increasingly embrace congregationalism in our historic connectional and covenant community.

We are beginning to embrace a set of practices and policies in The United Methodist Church that may lead our congregations to become increasingly independent from the denomination. Some people feel that our denomination as a whole is finished and that the best we can do is save the most promising congregations. That notion is a form of battlefield triage, saving the strongest and letting the dying die. Pastors and leaders of self-proclaimed "survival" congregations set a course that steers them clear of the denominational shore line, keeping them alone in a wide sailing lane.

## The Signs of Creeping Congregationalism Are All Around Us

We have encouraged the cloth of the independent entrepreneur as contemporary garb for clergy. We celebrate gospel "lone rangers" as role models. Often, those pastors define themselves as being "outside" the denomination to maintain their independence and freedom. Believing that the connection holds them back, they keep the denomination at arms' length and pay apportionments to keep the denomination "off their backs."

These leaders talk about ministry delayed and mission opportunities ignored because the denomination drains money that could be better spent at home. Every year, their voices grow louder at annual conference.

The congregations we admire are—more often than not—the growing, dynamic, and independent "megachurches" that seem to operate with the freedom to do what they please. We are tempted by their independence and congregational polity. They operate *unconnected* and *untied,* and their successes are impressive.

Some pastors of newly established congregations seem to want to disguise the *United Methodist* part of their names. They want to be viewed as free-standing congregations independent of the denomination—*untied* from its structures and restrictions.

Before we embrace congregationalism, however, we need to consider some important issues.

### Chapter 1: Current Reality in The United Methodist Church

**There is no future for the local United Methodist church apart from the denomination.**

As the denomination goes, so goes the local congregation. United Methodist pastors must take responsibility for the denomination, engage its leaders, and work for transformation that stretches from the bishop's office to the local church. In our system, when a pastor leaves his or her appointment, the *system* moves in to appoint the next pastor. The *system* has the power to support or undo what a local church pastor has spent years accomplishing. To ignore that power and possibility is unwise in our system.

Unless a pastor is willing to cross a final bridge by trying to make his or her church an independent congregation *outside* the *system*, he or she has a major stake in the connection. It's the truth about who we are. We can't cross those bridges that lead to the land of independent congregationalism, nor can we dismiss the power of our system. Rather than turning away, we must turn to embrace and build a new connectionalism for the twenty-first century.

**Is the connected community a contract community or a covenant community?**

A contract can be negotiated. It can be amended or dismissed when one or both parties agree that the relationship is no longer binding or important.

A covenant is forever. We become part of a covenant community, not by the power of negotiation, but by the gift and grace of the covenant and the One who calls us to it. We enter a covenant community, not with the idea that we can change the terms, but with the expectation that we will live and work with others in the covenant community, making the interests and well-being of the whole community the center of our life's work.

Is the United Methodist connection a contract or a covenant community? Can we negotiate our way in or out as suits our individual purposes? Can we declare our interests to be the narrow interests of our congregation and push away the demands of the larger connection? Or does the covenant that connects call for something else?

*March 1991*

## Apportionments

Each year, the annual conference informs each United Methodist congregation of its best estimate of that congregation's fair share of the cost of administering the ministry of the church beyond the congregation. All United Methodists participate in the church's world-wide ministry through a system of *apportionments*.

It should be a privilege, a joy, to give to such a vast array of ministry offerings. We give because we care. We care because we have been cared for. Maybe that's too simple theologically, but it's what I learned early in life, and it has worked for me. Moreover, I have seen it work for thousands of others.

> *We have lost the joy of giving. Giving must again become something to celebrate.*

People love to share, to help, to build new possibilities when they know the needs and can envision a better future. Giving is not a duty; it is a joy. Giving is something to celebrate!

We have a problem in The United Methodist Church today. Giving has become a chore. It is promoted as a duty, and it is responded to that way. I never hear anyone talking about the joys of giving in The United Methodist Church. I never hear anybody talking enthusiastically about the outreach ministry of the church. I rarely hear anyone expressing gratitude to annual conference or general church agencies for the work they do to extend the local church's ministry. I never hear anybody arguing that the church can do more. Am I in the wrong places?

To laypeople, apportionments seem like taxes. To clergy, apportionments seem like a lot of hard work to raise money. In the worst circumstances, apportionments seem like penalties or the "costs of doing business."

We cannot continue this way. We are not getting enough money to run the church at its present level. More importantly, we have lost the joy of giving. Giving must again become something to celebrate.

The financial giving system of the church is not working well. If everybody is displeased with the present system, it cannot be working well. However, blaming someone is not the answer. It is unfair to blame our people or our pastors.

In a day when fewer and fewer people care about preserving institutions and when more and more people give vast resources to causes they do care about, the present apportionment system produces less and less income for the denomination. Moreover, the apportionment system treats people as if they were sheep to be regimented, rather than disciples to be sent out in faithfulness.

The financial system—the whole system—is not working well. We can do better.

Could some leadership group in the church take the responsibility of looking at our system and figuring out how to improve it for the twenty-first century? Maybe the Council of Bishops could initiate the effort. The General Board of Discipleship could provide staff support and the learnings we have developed through research in stewardship, lay ministry, and financial giving. Other agencies could help too. Our congregations and annual conferences would welcome the opportunity to participate in improving the present system.

The task is not a simple one. Some have proposed that we change the term "apportionments" to "connectional ministries" or another more "missional" sounding title. What do you think? Will a change in terminology improve the present system? Will it make it more participatory, more open? Will it increase United Methodists' confidence in those who administer the denomination's resources? Will changing a few words make us want to celebrate United Methodist benevolences?

I don't think so. We would simply be tampering with the financial system—not improving it. For many reasons—some of them political—improving the financial system will not be easy. We need a system change—not a name change; and we need leaders—real ones!

*September 1991*

## *A Room with No Windows*

It was nine o'clock on a Tuesday morning. A dark, windowless room in a Chicago hotel was the setting for a meeting in which the General Council on Ministries was asking a committee of the General Council on Finance and Administration for a six percent annual increase in funding for the seven general program agencies of The United Methodist Church during the 1993-96 quadrennium.

The discussion was vitally interesting to those involved.

The General Council on Ministries' representatives talked about the program agencies' needs for increased funds to keep up with inflation and to maintain the work of the general church. Theirs was one perspective; their focus was the work of the general church.

The representatives of the General Council on Finance and Administration had a different perspective. They considered how much money could be raised for general church apportionments in the next few years. (Several of them are conference treasurers who believe, for the most part, that United Methodists are close to the limit in giving.)

Around the perimeter of the windowless room were the general secretaries of the program agencies. Theirs was a third perspective. They thought about their staffs and the programs of their agencies as they asked for more funds. They had to consider the need to raise salaries, avoid layoffs, fund new programs, and continue present ones. They looked on anxiously as the overhead projector failed. Was it an omen? Many of the general secretaries believed that more money could be raised if annual conferences and local church leaders would promote World Service funding with increased vigor.

As I sat in that meeting, my thoughts turned to the United Methodist people in the pews of 38,000 congregations. These people love God and want to be faithful disciples. They are not selfish. They give liberally—even sacrificially—when they are moved by a need; that is, when they own a need and when they own the church's response to it. "What is the psychological impact of what we are doing on people who feel they have no control over their own ministry?" asked one of the members of the group mentioned above.

In the room with no windows, three very different perspectives were heard. The representatives are loving and compassionate people. Their discussion, however, did not help them make a decision (which eventually was determined to be a 4.2 percent increase in funding each year for the four-year period).

I wondered as I sat there, "How can we possibly make the best decision, meeting in a room with no windows?" Without windows, we could not see people. When we cannot see people, we tend not to hear them.

If we had windows where our budget decisions are made, we would see:
- scores of congregations scrambling to find mission projects to support that will put them in personal relationships with people in other places;

- hundreds of churches and thousands of United Methodist individuals contributing hundreds of thousands of dollars to independent missions because they lack trust in their own denomination's benevolence system;
- United Methodist people asking to be taught about the needs of all people to know and love God and their neighbors; people who want to be informed and consulted about their church's response;
- United Methodists open to receiving the gospel anew from people of different cultures—people learning to receive as well as to give.

The United Methodist Church is historically a connectional system. Representatives have long made the decisions about budgets, and people have responded. They have responded as they have heard the stories of victories won, of people receiving the gospel, of human suffering being relieved. Today, the stories are vague, clouded, and even suspect. We are a diverse church. Causes supported by some are abhorred by others. Some give because they trust the system; they always have. However, some people don't trust the system anymore.

Our connectional system was built on trust. If that system of trust is breaking down, we either have to rebuild the system and reestablish trust, or find a new basis for our sharing as a church.

The issue is not how much money we need or how much money we can raise. The issue is not why we are in a room with no windows. Rather, the real issues are:

- Who do we want to be as a United Methodist Church?
- What kind of financial system will revive the joy of giving for all the members of the diverse United Methodist constituency?
- How can we reestablish trust between those who give and those who administer the gifts?
- How can we get out of this room with no windows?

*December 1991*

## *Appointments*

I recently sat with the bishop and cabinet of a United Methodist annual conference and listened to them explain to two new district superintendents the steps in the appointment process for that annual conference.

I was fascinated from beginning to end by the:

- extensive attention given to each congregation that would receive a new pastor;
- careful search for the "right" pastor to be considered for the appointment;
- relative unimportance given to salary as a criterion;
- delicate steps to be followed by a district superintendent in bringing the prospective pastor and church together to see if a match is right and could be happily entered into by both.

It was clear to me that this cabinet had carefully examined all the processes that made up the appointment system in this annual conference. It had improved the processes that were flawed and was looking for ways to improve the system further.

I don't know how many conferences have similar appointment processes, but I now believe that many conferences have better systems than I had previously imagined.

However, everywhere I go, I still hear laypeople and pastors saying they aren't pleased with the results of the appointive system. As a matter of fact, I think we may be close to revolution in some places—revolution that may be started by either the laity or the clergy. The results of the system are not the results wanted by either group.

While talking with the bishop who had instituted the aforementioned appointment process, I realized that the problem is bigger than the appointment process alone. Effective leadership development begins with the candidacy process, through which congregations invite and develop people to listen for a call from God for full-time or part-time pastoral ministry. It continues with district and conference processes of recruitment, encouragement, and testing of gifts for leadership.

Next is the long and difficult task of preparing people for leadership in the church...

- of helping them find spiritual mentors to support them in their formation in the spirit;
- of training them in the tradition and experiences of the Christian church through the ages;
- of helping them learn how social organizations, such as the church, function; of helping people learn how to lead churches and how to change and improve them over time.

As we talked, the bishop and I realized that the appointment process is only as good as the whole system of the annual conference—including the recruitment and training of pastoral leaders—enables it to be. If the annual conference calls and develops loving people who live in the power of the Holy Spirit, who know the Christian heritage and understand the dynamics of congregational life, who are connected to their colleagues in a cooperative rather than a competitive way, and who have knowledge about the nature of the church, then the cabinet will have leaders who can be deployed in congregations to lead the transformation of people, churches, and whole communities.

The United Methodist Church is big, multilayered, and decentralized in decision making; but it is a system. The parts have to fit together to form a whole that is focused and aligned to achieve the mission God has given it. Moreover, the system has to have able leaders at every level and in every place.

We do not have that now. It is not because the appointment system is not working—although that may be a major part of the problem in many places. It is not because the cabinets are not doing their best, and it is not because our pastors are not trying. We do not have good leaders at all levels because our system is not good enough in all its parts and in its total functioning to give us leaders who are appropriate for the task.

This bishop, cabinet, and conference leadership team have decided to work on the whole system in their annual conference over the next four to eight years. The bishop and cabinet will lead the effort, and I and my colleagues at the General Board of Discipleship will watch and assist where possible. We don't know too much yet about what this effort will embrace, but we expect them to pay attention to:

- the yearning of people to know and love God;
- the core process of faith development in congregations;
- the recruitment of all the clergy and laity of the annual conference to participate in the improvement effort;
- and the alignment of the entire system of the annual conference to achieve their vision for the church.

*January 1992*

## Impressions of the 1992 General Conference

I returned numb—both psychologically and physically—from the 1992 General Conference. I'm sure many who were in Louisville, May 5-15, felt much the same way.

The role of the General Conference in The United Methodist Church is to clarify our theology, set direction, and establish the boundaries and rules for our life and work. That session of the General Conference did some of all that.

- **Theology.** In 1988, the General Conference gave us a new Theological Task Statement and a new hymnal. The 1992 Conference gave us a new *Book of Worship* and a study document on baptism. It restated our denominational positions on abortion and homosexuality.

- **Direction.** The 1992 General Conference demonstrated continuing enthusiasm for the new United Methodist University in Africa; created a new mission in the former Soviet Union; responded with vigor to new possibilities for reaching Hispanic and Native American people in the United States; initiated new directions in campus ministry and in outreach to older adults and to those who are hearing-impaired; and asked the church to respond boldly to drug abuse, poverty, and violence in our society.

- **Boundaries and Rules.** The General Conference established a new health insurance system for clergy and lay workers, decided that the General Board of Global Ministries should move its headquarters out of New York, gave the Puerto Rico Conference the authority to become autonomous, set a budget for the next four years (approximately a ten percent increase), and fussed and fretted with scores of "shalls" and "shoulds" to keep the *Book of Discipline* tidy and orderly.

My observations from the back row are several:

*Our connectional system still works.* It has been bruised and battered and partially dismantled, particularly at congregational and conference levels, but it still is in place in the general church. It gets ugly sometimes. It is sorely tested when many major issues evenly divide the delegates. Further, it is difficult for a thousand people to move boldly together to seize new opportunities for ministry. However, the connectional system is still functioning and is crying out for reaffirmation, revitalization, and improvement.

*United Methodists are political and sometimes manipulative with other United Methodists.* On the other hand, United Methodists are open in dialogue about racism, classism, and sexism. Whatever hard issues are facing society, United Methodists discuss those issues publicly as they arise. We clearly do not agree about abortion, homosexuality, militarism, and advocacy for human rights; but at least we don't remove these issues from our agenda.

*General Conference is a time for letting the people speak.* The bishops, some of whom serve as presiding officers, sit on the stage without voice or vote; the general secretaries sit on the back row without voice or vote. For two weeks, laity and clergy elected by those who fill the pews and pulpits of the denomination make decisions. General Conference is a time for those elected to lead the church to listen to the people. I hope we heard them!

*There was a distracting mood in the 1992 General Conference.* Some called it meanness; others called it anger, spite, or revenge. Those of us who work in the general program agencies felt that we were viewed as unruly, unrepentant, and scheming offspring. At times during this General Conference, it seemed as if the delegates had been instructed by their churches and annual conferences to "go and protect us from the general church." Such attitudes were sometimes embarrassing.

From start to finish, it seemed as if many General Conference delegates had come with their minds made up, or that many showed particular zeal to push their own causes. Each morning, we were greeted at the convention center by people representing one caucus or another. Representatives of very conservative groups stood next to representatives from the Methodist Federation for Social Action, the Women's Caucus, and Affirmation ( an organization supporting gay men and lesbians) as they distributed their daily information sheets. I often wondered if the groups talked to one another when pedestrian traffic was slow.

Perhaps the most distressing phenomenon to me was the regionalism demonstrated between the southern jurisdictions in the United States and the northern and western jurisdictions. The ugliest part of the whole conference occurred when regionalism broke open in a discussion regarding the formula for apportioning delegates to General Conference.

*United Methodists are people who have little in common—except a "desire to flee from the wrath to come and be saved from our sins."* We also have a common ancestry in both the human predicament and the Wesleyan heritage of faith in the grace of God. We are truly a diverse people. Just now, we are so mired in the human predicament that we sometimes wonder whether God is capable of or amenable to saving us—lifting us to a higher plane of faithfulness and accountability.

I am hopeful, not because we can deliver ourselves from the mire, but because God can and is doing that even now!

*July 1992*

THINK ABOUT IT...

## *The Doctor and the Church*

The film *The Doctor* portrays a heart surgeon who became a patient because he had a malignant tumor on his larynx.

Part of the film is amusing as we watch the doctor learn what it's like to be a patient...

- filling out countless forms;
- waiting;
- wearing hospital gowns that leave patients vulnerable in the rear;
- dealing with seemingly uncaring doctors;
- having colleagues treat you like a sick person.

> *To improve the quality of any organization's service, it is necessary to have knowledge of the customer.*

The doctor's experience was a rather unpleasant way for him to get customer knowledge, to learn what his institution was really producing and how it was perceived by patients. However, to improve the quality of any organization's service, it is necessary to have knowledge of the customer.

While waiting for his daily radiation treatment, the doctor met a young woman who was dying of a level-four brain tumor. She also visited the hospital for daily treatments. She didn't like the doctor's desire for special treatment and told him so. He knew that she was right, and they became friends.

One day, the doctor told the woman that his father had once treated a patient with a level-four brain tumor. That patient was now a grandfather, he assured her.

The next day, the young woman asked the doctor not to lie to her—not to give her false hope. When you're dying, you are searching for hope—more than anything else in the world—but false hope is not helpful. The doctor admitted then that he knew of no patient who had ever survived a level-four brain tumor.

Parts of the institutional church are dying today—congregations in changing communities, congregations that have held on to the past. Bookstores continue to display books with methods and "how-tos." Congregational consultants continue to tell people how to relate their congregations to the community and how to grow and become strong.

The churches are crying, "Don't lie to us! We need hope, but don't lie to us."

When will we understand that annual conferences, general agencies, and outside consultants cannot give congregations miracle cures with quick fixes and preset programs? Such cures are not helpful; they don't give real hope. None of those "cures" can substitute for trained and knowledgeable, long-term leadership within the congregation.

"Be my friend," said the young woman in the movie. "Tell me what you know. Help me get information. But don't lie to me!"

The doctor was not a good patient. He was selfish, and he alienated his wife, his partners, his hospital colleagues, and others. When he realized that his life could be different and tried to reach out to people, he didn't know how.

On the night before the young woman died, she wrote a letter to the doctor, hoping that he would receive it before his surgery. He didn't, but the letter still made its point. In the letter, she told him a story:

> *There was a farmer who worked hard to keep the birds away from his fields. Later he decided he wanted the birds to come back. He went out in the middle of his fields and waved his arms, beckoning them to come. But they would not come because they were frightened by this "new scarecrow." "Dear Jack," the woman wrote, "Just let down your arms, and we will all come to you."*

Thousands of United Methodist congregations want to be loving, to reach out to people, and to help people be a part of the Body of Christ. If these congregations could just relax, put down their arms, and work on the basics!

*September 1992*

THINK ABOUT IT...

## Sometimes You Can See Only from the Inside

A friend and former pastor told me about the Christmas Day service at his church. He said that the big attendance was on Christmas Eve night, but that he liked to have a service on Christmas Day too. One year, about sixty people gathered down front in the large sanctuary on Christmas morning for a service of Holy Communion. Included in the small congregation was a couple the pastor had never seen before. They observed, but did not participate.

They left immediately after the service—before the pastor could greet them. A few days later, the pastor saw the woman in the grocery store. He approached her and thanked her for coming. She said that she and her husband were Jewish, had decided they wanted to know something about the Christian faith, and thought the best time to learn would be during one of Christianity's holy days. They came to church on Christmas Day—when Christians tend to stay home and celebrate a secular Christmas. You have to be an insider to know that Christians do the religious celebrating the night before Christmas. It's not better that way, but it is the way we do it.

*Sometimes you can see only from the inside.*

The primary focus of our United Methodist ministry is people—people who come and those who may come. The primary place of ministry is where people live. The primary place of preparation for ministry is the congregation, where people gather from various communities.

The basic system for supporting United Methodist ministry is the annual conference. It is here that our most fundamental implementation decisions are made, and it is from the annual conference that congregational leaders are deployed.

The General Conference establishes the mission—theological and social—for the churches and establishes norms for carrying out the mission.

If you have never been to a United Methodist annual conference or to General Conference, you might be surprised by the agenda. If you expect the discussion to center on the focus of ministry (people) or the primary places of ministry (communities and congregations), or understanding and implementing our denomination's mission, you will find little of that.

In earlier times, Methodists did discuss such matters. In Mr. Wesley's day, people concentrated on:

- what to teach.
- how to teach.
- what to do.

However, times are different now; and there are too many other things to do in these meetings. You ask why?

*Sometimes you can see only from the inside.*

*November 1992*

# Organizations in Decline

I have recently attended some churches that are vital, alive, and in full ascendancy. Just being in those churches and savoring their vibrancy reminded me of the tell-tale signs of other churches—churches in decline. I realized that what we often see and hear in our old-line denominations are classic indicators of organizations in decline.

The following indicators of decline apply to churches (and to other organizations):

- The organization is aimless. It has no clear sense of movement, journey, or direction.
- Goals—if they exist at all—are short-term and about relatively insignificant objectives.
- Leaders give increasing attention to planning and finding the "right" methods.
- Leaders *talk* about doing evaluation, but do *little actual evaluation*.
- The organization has great faith in mergers (of classes, congregations, conferences), which are rationalized as regrouping strategies, rather than as retreat measures.
- People tend to draw circles around their special interests and declare them to be sacred.
- Leaders and members take few risks.
- The organization values rational thinking; intuition is undeveloped.
- People cannot talk about creating something new without talking about adding to or "redeveloping the old." (For example, someone might say: "We want to start new congregations—*and* redevelop old ones."
- Leaders talk about visioning without understanding that they can't move from where they are without adequately defining current reality and dealing with what holds them there.
- The organization's values are general, hazy, and don't lead anywhere. There is lots of talk about sincerity, commitment, loyalty, good communication. There is more concern about the "shape of the table" than about the content of the discussion.
- Dissidents are isolated.
- People respond to problems by finding someone to blame.
- There is rampant tightening of the rules, which leads to an increased breaking of the rules.
- Leaders hold on to projects at any cost—if those projects produce income.

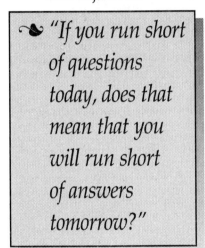

*"If you run short of questions today, does that mean that you will run short of answers tomorrow?"*

- The organization has conflicting strategies for raising funds, without seeing the conflicts. For example, churches might be sending these conflicting messages:

  *"God expects a tithe—but if you can't do that, pick a percentage and make it the rule of your giving."*

  *"Give out of gratefulness to God—the church needs your money to survive."*
- "Leaders" confuse leadership with keeping order.
- People believe, "If it's not broken, let's not even think about it." Another prevailing attitude is, "When you can't do it easily or naturally, force it."

Perhaps the most invisible and insidious indicator of decline is inertia. Recently a friend, who is a management consultant to many kinds of organizations, related his experience of attending a weekend seminar at a large United Methodist church. He was impressed with what the leaders had done, but was unpleasantly surprised to find that they had no bold new plans for the future. He said that they had lots of answers, but no questions.

I wonder, "If you run short of questions today, does that mean that you will run short of answers tomorrow?"

*January 1994*

CHAPTER 1: CURRENT REALITY IN THE UNITED METHODIST CHURCH

## *Bloated with Bureaucracy*

The August 29, 1994, issue of *Newsweek* told an amazing story of change. The seemingly unstoppable rise to prominence of the Japanese automobile industry in the 1980s had halted. Riding a wave of higher quality and value, Toyota, Nissan, and Honda were highly profitable until the worldwide recession hit in 1992. These companies were making and selling up to 20 percent fewer cars in 1994 than in the peak years. Many factors account for the changes, and it is possible that a rebound will occur.

During the "feast days," these companies added plants and equipment, showrooms and salespeople, and research and marketing capabilities. The costs of those additions remain with them. Money borrowed during those days continues to require interest payments, and maintenance costs are still required for underused buildings and equipment. "The industry employs 20,000 more permanent workers than it needed in 1985 to turn out the same number of vehicles." In sum, the leaner times of the present show up the "bureaucratic bloat" of the good times.

Businesses and organizations of all sorts are facing similar situations. Over time, they have increased their overhead and have fewer resources left for pursuing their mission. As a result, the cost per unit of product or service is excessive.

Another contemporary example is the airline industry. Southwest Airlines and a few other small "upstarts" focus on moving passengers and avoid many of the costs that burden the older, major airlines. American, United, and the like can't compete. The overhead they have amassed over the years causes their costs to sometimes double those of the newer, more focused companies.

Knowledgeable observers of the church today recognize the "bureaucratic bloat" in their own organizations. The cost of maintaining the older denominations—including Protestant, Roman Catholic, and Orthodox churches—greatly exceeds the cost of maintaining independent congregations, para-church groups, and emerging networks of congregations and mission service organizations. The latter are leaner and freer.

The United Methodist Church is the master of overhead—at every level. It was natural to accumulate it, but that doesn't make it any less costly. It has been 200 years in the making, and its necessity has now been justified many times over by those of us who have come to like it or benefit from it.

Consider, for example, real estate. The resources we have in land and buildings to house congregations and conference and general church offices are massive. Yet how many are partially used or used for just a few hours each week? At what point in our development as a denomination did pastors give up the horse (for spending time with the people) for an office?

An article in *Fortune* (September 5, 1994) magazine calls real estate "the last big gold mine on the balance sheet." The article notes that "IBM, General Electric, Eastman Kodak, AT&T, and Mobil each has plans to save more than $100 million in space costs over the next few years" by consolidating offices and managing property differently. "AT&T could easily save $1 million a day." Most of us in the church cannot imagine using buildings differently.

Consider how many pastors serve The United Methodist Church. How many do we need? I believe several thousand fewer. While our membership, attendance, and number of churches have fallen significantly in the last quarter century, the number of pastors under appointment has stayed the same. We are over-deployed in small congregations and under-deployed in large ones. Is there any wonder that we are getting fewer large ones?

Think about how many meetings we attend in the church. (If this one needs explanation, someone else will have to do it. I have to go to a meeting.)

The above are the most visible ways we burden ourselves with overhead. We also have official or commonly accepted practices and procedures that take time and kill our passion. There are rules that order our work and inhibit creativity and innovation. There are coordination processes that serve as rationales for limiting initiative and saying *No* to the unusual.

There is no one to blame. The piling on of processes and procedures is normal for all organizations. What is frightening is how quickly the processes can overburden an organization. It took scarcely more than a decade for that to happen to Japanese auto companies.

The church groups being formed today will lose their ability to serve tomorrow, just as the mainline denominations earlier lost their edge. The future belongs to those who have the foresight to see it with new lenses and new mental models and who have the flexibility to act quickly and appropriately.

Perhaps The United Methodist Church could position itself to lead into the future. We could act now to design a new, parallel system for opening up, listening to different people, and risking what we have. Those of us at the General Board of Discipleship are finding that there are a few bishops and conferences and a few pastors and congregations out there who are daring enough to try.

They will have no safety nets, no lifeboats if they tire of the swim. They will have no protection against the inevitable restraining forces that will block them. However, for those willing to take the risk, there is the possibility of new life and new measures of faithfulness.

*October 1994*

CHAPTER 1: CURRENT REALITY IN THE UNITED METHODIST CHURCH

## *Lofty Visions and Continued Decline*

Do you remember learning in basic science courses about how organisms grow? Cells divide and multiply. Many organizations grow the same way. It has long been the basic pattern of denominational growth: People from one or more churches become the nucleus for a new congregation. Historically, in the United Methodist denomination, the same growth cycle took place in conferences. As they became too large to be manageable, or as greater outreach was possible through dividing and multiplying, more conferences were created. That pattern continues today in United Methodism in Africa and the Philippines.

*If division is the method of growth, what is the role of merger in the church?*

More specifically, what is the role of conference mergers in The United Methodist Church? Let's look at some important issues:

> *Are we applying a quick remedy to denominational difficulties with conference mergers? Are we removing the symptoms of trouble too soon and taking away the option of identifying the real issues and dealing with them appropriately?*

• Why are we getting so many mergers and why are we hearing discussions about several more? Are conferences merging out of strength or out of weakness?

• What should be the larger context for considering whether conferences merge? Survival? Saving money? Reaching more people? Reaching people born since mid-century? Transforming believers into disciples?

• Are mergers a method of combining two or more conferences when one or more are facing serious difficulties? Is it possible that, by merging, the conferences will never face their difficulties adequately?

• Are conference mergers an informal (perhaps even unconscious) affirmation of a decade-long period of numerical decline that is projected to continue into the future? Are we creating a self-fulfilling prophesy? Are conferences merging simply to buy time? Does the rush to merge signal a rush to save face, cut costs, and die gracefully as a denomination?

I am concerned about our motives for mergers, our expectations, and our actual results.

Now, I know that there are many reasons given for conference mergers:

• To have adequate resources for ministry.
• To give the bishop a one-point charge.
• To provide greater flexibility in appointments.
• To begin anew and create a vessel for ministry for the present and future.

There are many more reasons for mergers. I fully support the four goals listed above. If merger would give a high probability of accomplishing those four goals, I would be the biggest supporter of mergers. In the present day, conferences are too complex and require too much leadership—particularly in a connectional system—for us to continue multiple-conference episcopal areas. Moreover, we do need opportunities to rebuild and start anew with sufficient size and resources to move boldly into the future.

Watching conferences merge over the last one-third of a century, however, and serving as a consultant in planning for several mergers, I wonder if *we are holding lofty visions and getting continued decline.*

- Are we creating new conference systems with new energy for moving in new ways?
- Are we positing new visions and designing new processes to move toward those visions?
- Are we, through these mergers, improving the day-to-day ministry in our churches?
- Are we improving our processes of recruiting, testing, training, nurturing, credentialing, and deploying pastors?
- Do we have evidence that mergers have appreciably improved our ability to reach out and receive people into the Christian community, relate them to God, nurture them in the faith, and send them out to live as faithful disciples?

—OR—

- Are we consuming people's energy to do something that as many as half of them don't want?
- Are we breaking up long-standing relationships and communities of faith without replacing them with more loving communities and more faithful ministry?

Perhaps the above questions grow out of my jaundiced perspective. I hope so. I do not want to make a case against conference mergers, but I do want to raise some important questions. I want to be sure we have an adequate conceptual framework for proposing mergers, debating them, and advocating for or opposing them. However, the most significant question I want to raise is a different one: *"Is conference merger a hidden factor in our ongoing denominational decline?"*

A loving daughter nursed her aged father during the long months of deteriorating health that preceded his death. On the last day of his life, he had difficulty breathing. As his gasps for breath became more urgent, the daughter gave him oxygen so that he wouldn't have to work so hard to breathe. The doctor explained later that the oxygen had hastened the man's death. It took away the need for his body to mobilize its forces to get oxygen to sustain life. The remedy interrupted the natural life-giving forces of the body.

Are we, similarly, applying a quick remedy to denominational difficulties with conference mergers? Are we removing the symptoms of trouble too soon and taking away the option of identifying the real issues and dealing with them appropriately? When we fail to deal with the real issues in the former conference systems, we may get new forms of the same issues in the new conference system.

Clearly, mergers are a fact of life today in every area of our lives—business, industry, health care, education, and more. A November 28, 1994, *Fortune* article entitled "The New Merger Boom" carried the headline: "New combinations are reshaping America's largest industries, with consequences for all. Shareholders could be the big losers."

The author, Terence Pare, believes that for the shareholders of the acquiring companies "the news is not all good."

> *"Many recent mergers have produced nothing but headaches and disappointment..."*
>
> *"Asked to name just one big merger that has lived up to expectations, Leon Cooperman, the former co-chairman of Goldman Sachs' investment policy committee, answers, 'I'm sure that there are success stories out there, but at this moment I draw a blank.'*
>
> *...After assessing U.S. deals conducted from the turn of the century through the 1980s, Dennis Mueller of the University of Vienna summarily concluded: 'On average, mergers are bad.'"*

In industry, the motives for mergers are diverse and cover the spectrum of legitimacy. The same is true in the church. I am not questioning all mergers. I do question the seemingly "simple solution" that we have found for not dealing adequately with our present condition.

No blame here. Just some questions.

*February 1995*

## Exclusive Territories

Martin Marty quotes John Ralston Saul, a Canadian novelist and essayist, who in a forthcoming lexicon defines a university as "a place in which a civilization's knowledge is divided up into exclusive territories." Saul goes on to comment:

> "The principal occupation of the academic community is to invent dialects sufficiently hermetic to prevent knowledge from passing between territories. By maintaining a constant flow of written material among the specialists of each group, academics are able to assert the acceptable technique of communication intended to prevent communications. This, in turn, establishes a standard that allows them to dismiss those who seek to communicate through generally accessible language as dilettantes, deformers, or popularizers." (Context, January 1, 1995, quoting Wilson Quarterly, Summer)

> *What if the church were defined as a multifaceted community of people who are seeking God?*

Couldn't our church structure be similarly characterized? One might define the church as *"a place in which religious programs, emphases, and events are divided up among separate and exclusive committees and work areas—education, worship, evangelism, stewardship, lay ministry, social concerns, missions."* Each has its own goals and basis for legitimacy, methods and language, defenders, and claims to primacy. Church professionals focus on one or another function. Congregations, conferences, and whole denominations structure around them. Seminaries have professorships in most of these disciplines. Authors publish books in these subject areas, and fund raisers seek gifts in the name of one or the other church functions.

If the above definition of church is an accurate description of reality in United Methodism, then we are failing to reap the benefits of *synergy*—parts and processes working together for the good of the whole. What we have now is *suboptimization*, and we are paying attention only to penultimate ends. A car's engine, wheels, and transmission may all be in good working order, but if those parts are not connected and working together, the car can't take you where you want to go.

At some point, we United Methodists will have to question whether or not our functional categories are helpful. These labor divisions may indicate that the church has moved away from paying attention to the historic disciplines of the Christian faith (what Wesley called the "means of grace") and has substituted a schema designed to keep us active, even if we are not productive.

Let's try some new definitions. What if a *university* were defined as a *multi-disciplinary setting for the pursuit of knowledge?* What if the *church* were defined as a *multifaceted community of people who are seeking God?*

The new definition of church would cause us in United Methodism to focus on watching for God's action in the world, on loving God, and on bringing our lives into alignment with God's being among us. We would concentrate on faithful attendance at the Lord's Supper, on prayer, on study of the word, on fasting, on Christian conferencing, on acts of mercy. We would pay more attention to Wesley's admonition to "Do No Harm."

United Methodists are not renegades. We have always sought to exhibit the core of Christian belief and responsibility. However, we are approaching the margins of responsiveness and accountability. Our division of labor is no longer working. Many see the harm in our choosing up sides and allegiances.

Our categories are the traditional ones. They are important *aspects* of the core process (primary task). The problem is that each function has become an end in itself. The functions are not seen as part of the primary task of reaching and receiving people, relating them to God, developing them as disciples, and sending them out to change the world. We have lost the understanding that each function depends on the others. Each is significant only in relation to the task that runs through them all.

There are really only two corporate activities that the church must do: provide transcendent worship and offer small groups. The first fulfills the First Commandment of Jesus; the second anchors the Second Commandment. Both activities help us to be faithful to both commandments. However, in many churches, committee meetings to plan programs dominate the activities. Many church leaders ask, "What things do you do when you're a church?" Then they do what they think they are expected to do instead of paying attention to the people who are seeking God.

It is time for United Methodists to attend to people (including ourselves) and their (our) search for God. That attention will entail learning, celebrating, repenting, forgiving, inviting people to follow Jesus, living as grateful recipients of God's creation, seeking to develop pure hearts, serving others, relieving human suffering, and proclaiming the good news to the ends of the earth.

I believe that paying attention to people's yearning for God is different from paying attention to programming.

*March 1995*

## We Don't Need This

The General Council on Ministries (GCOM) submitted a proposal to the 1992 General Conference asking that body to request that GCOM conduct a listening and visioning study across the church and then recommend structural changes based on the study. The General Conference did make that request; now GCOM has a mandate to offer the church a new structure.

In early January 1995, GCOM released its first proposal for structural change throughout the church. It called for a radical new structure for congregations, conferences, and the general church. Supposedly, the proposed structure was developed out of information gained in the listening processes. However, it is not clear how one process led to the other.

> *The gospel of Jesus Christ has the power to change lives and to transform the world...To focus on the transformation of the church in order to transform the church is to achieve no change.*

For raw data to be helpful, it must be processed through testing into knowledge. Using information gained from the listening surveys, persons can form and test theories. The theories then, which *may* be confirmed by the testing (or invalidated or improved), can lead persons to expect certain results from particular actions. For example, we might be able to say—with reasonable confidence—that if we have fewer committees and task forces, we can free more people for direct ministries of service. On the other hand, we might find that the opposite is true. How can we know until we form theories and test them? Before we restructure again, shouldn't we test our ideas before we act? We need to ask two very important questions:

(1) How will we know that any change is an improvement?

(2) On what basis can we predict that this proposed change will lead to the improvements and results we want?

However, we must first address a prior question, "What are we trying to accomplish by this change?"

The General Council on Ministries' proposal for restructure states that the vision that emerges from the church-wide listening study is a vision for a "vibrant church." If a vibrant church is indeed what we want, how do we define "vibrant" and what are the indicators that a church is not "vibrant"? Even if we could adequately define "vibrant," we would still have a problem. Any vision that focuses on the institutional church is penultimate and does not have the power to change people and the world. The only vision for the church that can have life-changing power is one that goes beyond a focus on the institutional church to a focus on people and the world and God's transformation.

My colleagues and I have come to believe some basic assumptions about the church and the power of the gospel:

(1) The gospel of Jesus Christ has the power to change lives and to transform the world.

(2) The church, which is people gathered in community around Christ, has been endowed with this gospel, this life-changing power.

(3) The church, when focused on people and the transformation of the world, can be an agent of the world's transformation.

(4) Sometimes the church itself needs transformation, and the power of the gospel again is sufficient.

(5) The church, when focused on the transformation of the world, can be an agent of its own transformation.

(6) Whether the aim of the church is the transformation of the world or the transformation of the church itself, the church, when focused on the transformation of people and the world, can be an agent of that transformation.

(7) To focus on the transformation of the church in order to transform the church is to achieve no change.

> *Our task is to focus on people and the work of the church rather than on the church itself.*

For the last one third of the twentieth century, The United Methodist Church has been focusing attention on itself (on how to become "vibrant"). Everything we have tried has resulted in no change or ineffective change. Without evidence to the contrary, we can expect that the proposed new structure will give us more of the same.

*The system is designed for the results it is getting. If we want different results we will have to redesign the system. But to redesign the system, we will have to be clear about who we are, what we do, and the benefits we bring to the world.*

Our task then is to focus on people and the work of the church rather than on the church itself. As the church works on transformation beyond itself, it becomes a vibrant church. As it works on its own transformation in order to become a vibrant church, it continues dying.

I don't want to examine here the strengths and weaknesses of the GCOM proposal. Without clarity about what is to be accomplished by any structure, one structure is as good as another; the old structure is as good as the projected one. Without clarity, we cannot evaluate any proposal.

Consider these ideas:

(1) Let's set our sights (our vision) beyond the church itself.
(2) Let's be as clear and specific as we can about our vision so that we can determine if we are achieving it and what can help us achieve it.
(3) Let's be reasonably certain that a change will be an improvement before we spend thousands of hours and hundreds of thousands of dollars bringing about the change.
(4) Let's build and test some theories regarding a system that can deliver our vision so that we can be sure that the new system can do what the old one could not.

I believe that *radical change is needed* in our United Methodist Church system (including the General Board of Discipleship). We do need to act promptly to discover how we can bring about change effectively.

I also believe that people can't have an adequate vision in any organization without appropriate leadership. At all levels of the church, we need *learning leaders* who will listen to people and then state the people's visions in the context of God's vision as given by Christ and the whole experience and tradition of the church. Maybe we should be focusing our attention initially on leadership rather than on structure.

The discussions and debate around the GCOM structure proposal and others that will be offered across the church may slow us down, sap our energy, and make us even more impotent as a place of spiritual formation and transformation.

The best restructure we could do in United Methodism might be to discard all structures that help us *plan* to seek God or *plan* to do ministry. Instead, we could focus on the simple Wesleyan *means of grace* (Bible study, prayer, fasting, celebration of the Lord's Supper, spiritual conferencing, and acts of mercy and justice). If we change our focus, maybe God will give us new marching orders and a new system for falling into formation and moving out.

Oh yes! Wesley always talked about practicing these historic spiritual disciplines by first admonishing *"Do no harm."* Brother John, maybe you need to start us there one more time!

*April 1995*

# CHAPTER 2:

## SYSTEMS, THE PRIMARY TASK OF THE CHURCH, AND THE PEOPLE WE SERVE

| | |
|---|---|
| Getting New Results Requires a New System | 28 |
| Blaming | 30 |
| Improving the System | 32 |
| Won't He Ever Learn! | 34 |
| Primary Task | 35 |
| Christian Community | 38 |
| More About Christian Community | 41 |
| Members and Customers | 43 |
| Evangelism | 46 |
| Wow! Was She Ever Wrong! | 48 |
| Marketing the Church | 50 |
| Let's Not Turn the Message Into Bait | 52 |
| Confusion About the Journey | 54 |
| A New Quest? Let's Focus on Essentials | 57 |

Think About It...

# Getting New Results Requires a New System

A certain farmer set a goal of plowing ten acres a day. Each morning, he hitched his mules to the plow and set off for the fields to turn the soil. No matter how hard he drove the mules or how well he had slept the night before, he could not plow more than five acres a day. The combination of the mules and the plow just would not stretch to achieve the desired result.

The farmer spent his evenings sharpening his plow, reworking the harness, and resting and feeding his mules. He prayed, scolded, schemed, and planned; but his results were always the same: five acres a day.

He traded mules, bought a new plow, and ordered a new harness for his team. He ordered books about plowing, enrolled in a training course, and practiced meditation; but all his efforts fell short. Nothing the farmer tried brought him any closer to his goal, because his system had a built-in result: five acres a day. The result was dictated by the system of mules, harness, man, and plow. *His system was designed for the results it got.*

The farmer's failure had nothing to do with lack of motivation, desire, or self-esteem. He got the maximum results from the system he used. Unless he changed his *system,* he could never achieve his goal.

### The Annual Conference Is a System

The annual conference is a system within The United Methodist Church that is made up of churches, leaders, structures, and resources designed to achieve specific results.

The results that today's annual conference leaders want may be more growth or greater vitality and effectiveness, but the *system* now in place is designed to achieve the results it gets—and nothing more.

### Change the System

Annual conference leaders may replace components of the organization, change leaders, call on persons to work harder, and offer training, but the outcome will not change. Unless the *system* is changed, nothing more can be expected.

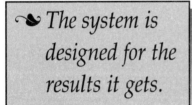

*The system is designed for the results it gets.*

The answer to the farmer's dilemma was for him to change his system. He needed a tractor or a larger plow to achieve his goal. Annual conference leaders, likewise, must change the system to achieve new results.

A first step toward achieving new results requires a shift away from "snapshot" thinking, or thinking that isolates critical components of the system and attempts change by concentrating on individual parts, rather than on understanding how the parts combine to create a system.

Our farmer focused on first one component, then another. He failed to see his system as a whole and realize that continued use of his system made it impossible for him to achieve the desired results.

Systems understanding is the first step toward attaining a new future. The system we have in place may belong to another era; it may no longer be capable of achieving the results we need and want for the twenty-first century. If we continue to work within the system we now have, making minor changes, adopting new programs, or passing resolutions, we will find ourselves with the same unacceptable results.

To get new results requires a new system. To get new results requires leaders of vision, courage, and imagination who will undertake the task of building for a new and challenging century.

*February 1991*

## Blaming

In one annual conference—I am told—the names of pastors whose congregations have not paid apportionments in full are read. One person who has observed this practice has commented, "The people in the pew feel that they are being treated like children; they feel belittled. They may or may not love their pastor deeply, but they don't like 'the conference' to make their pastor look bad. It feels like a personal affront, and it certainly does not feel like 'family.'"

> "In all situations, blaming inhibits effective action."

When things aren't going well, someone always gets blamed. Sometimes there is enough blame to pass around to many folks.

Blame is usually directed at "other" people, except when there is no possible "other" person who could be at fault. In such cases, blame is usually placed on a machine: "the car broke down," "the alarm didn't go off," "the plane was late."

It seems natural to blame. If an activity or process could clearly be improved, or if it is so bad that people are "turned off," it seems appropriate to blame someone or something. The problem is that blaming doesn't motivate people to act differently.

All of society does it. Management blames workers; workers blame management. The Democrats blame the Republicans, who respond in kind. Husbands and wives blame each other, as do parents and children, brothers and sisters.

It has always been so. Adam blamed Eve; Cain blamed Abel; the elder brother blamed the prodigal and his father. The Jews blamed Jesus; the Romans blamed the Jews. Blaming is so much a part of our culture, our world, and our very lives that we do not know how *not* to blame. When we can't place blame, it seems that "something is missing." Blaming diverts attention from ourselves and gives us something to talk about. It can even be enjoyable.

There are at least two problems that are inherent to blaming:

(1) Blaming focuses on the end of a process or system, rather than on improving the process that produced the undesirable results. It is easier to cry (blame) over spilled milk—or spilled oil in Alaska—than it is to improve the system that led to the spill.

(2) Blaming is un-Christian and unfair. "You have heard an eye for an eye…, but I say unto you…" As parents, as brothers or sisters, as supervisors, have we not contributed to the results that are reflected by our children, siblings, or employees?

The United Methodist Church today does not always work perfectly in all places at all times. As a matter of fact, with so many processes and subsystems not functioning at all (or functioning poorly), it is a wonder that any of it works well. At times and in some places, The United Methodist Church does work well. But through years of attrition, neglect, and change, primary processes have lost their power and ability to contribute effectively to that which we want for our church. One immediate problem is that we can't focus on improving or replacing the processes because we can't get beyond blaming those we have decided are responsible.

Outside the church, blaming sometimes leads to marital breakups, family estrangement, unemployment, even war. In all situations, blaming inhibits effective action.

Blaming has become vicious, hurtful, and destructive as the United Methodist system has slowly degenerated over many decades. Blaming is blocking our regeneration as a church. It is a sin that must be exorcised before we can begin the long task of repair and the search for newness of life.

I have been one of the guilty ones. I want to be part of the answer in the future. I'm working on it.

I have been trying to refrain from blaming others. It hasn't been easy. I have to work harder and longer to discern the real problems. Worse yet, sometimes the problems stem from something I did (or didn't do). I'd rather blame somebody!

*June 1991*

## Improving the System

Blaming is a "natural," enjoyable, and sinful thing we do to assuage our guilt and account for things around us that don't work well.

What are the alternatives to blaming? There are several:

*Do nothing.* "Maybe I can wait it out and let my successor deal with it." "This conference is not functioning very well, but it won't fall apart—probably—for several years. Besides, it is all I can do just to hold it together."

*Abandon the relationship or situation.* Get out while you can. "This relationship is not working. I will end it and seek a different one."

*Complain about how bad the situation is.* Most of us understand this alternative!

*A more effective alternative is to work to improve the processes of the organization.* I can work to improve that part for which I have responsibility, and I can seek out leaders at other places in the organization who will join the effort.

Members of the organization can do their part, but they can contribute only as much as the present system allows. Leaders, on the other hand, can manage the system so that its capacity is expanded and improved.

The role of leader in any organization is primarily to : (1) help the people establish a vision—or an aim—and (2) constantly improve the system and processes that will move the organization closer to the vision.

In the five miles between my house and office, there are twenty traffic lights and stop signs. As a driver, I cannot improve the traffic control system. The best I can do is drive the distance in a safe, courteous, lawful, and fuel-efficient way.

The city government, using traffic engineers, can do much more. As managers of the city, they have the authority and the resources to improve the traffic signals in a way that will control traffic in response to changing conditions. If they improve the traffic flow system, the daily commute will be improved for all drivers.

Today, the systems of The United Methodist Church are caught in a destructive spiral: The systems of the church produce leaders who are restrained from leading by the very systems that produced them. The systems, on the other hand, can be changed and improved only by the leaders that the systems have produced and sustained.

The United Methodist Church has many leaders. The three primary leadership groups are: (1) congregational lay leaders; (2) pastors; (3) bishops and cabinets.

To illustrate the leader—system-improvement dilemma, we must note that:

- To be effective, congregational lay leaders must be appropriately recruited, trained, deployed, and held accountable. The responsibility for these tasks belongs to pastors. However, pastors may not be deployed long enough in one church to carry out the leadership recruitment functions adequately. Moreover, they may not be trained adequately for the task of training and holding others accountable.

- Responsibility for recruiting, credentialing, training, deploying, and evaluating pastors belongs to the conferences.
- The conferences are led by bishops (tenure normally limited to eight years) and district superintendents (tenure limited to six years) who may not be adequately trained and prepared to manage the church's basic system (the conference). The (conference) *system* may not have helped them understand that improving the (conference) *system* and its processes is their primary role. The demands and expectations of the current denominational system leave no time for the long-term, primary task of leadership.

None of these leaders want to do an inadequate job. They do the best they can, but the system precludes their doing more.

Authority for change comes from those who are led. United Methodist members are crying for change—for leadership, guidance, and new possibilities. The tragedy is that the present United Methodist system allows only those voices that support the *status quo* to be heard. We have effectively shut out our one voice of accountability—the voice of our people who want more.

The easy response is to blame the leaders we put in office, but whom our processes restrain or—at best—do not prepare, encourage, and support.

The productive response is to come together as laity, clergy, and cabinet to work on our systems. Maybe the place to begin is the annual conference.

Who will call us together?

*July 1991*

THINK ABOUT IT...

## *Won't He Ever Learn?*

That kid! Won't he ever learn? Every year, it's the same thing. He makes good money, but he spends even more. At the end of the year, he is short again. The loan to pay his income tax is barely paid off by the end of the next year; then he has to borrow again.

A certain annual conference came up short last year also. It had never happened before to that degree. Fewer congregations are paying their apportionments in full. Some say that the membership decline is affecting giving to the church. Others say the potential for increasing giving is there, but that the church has not challenged people to give.

Whatever the reason, when the accounts were added in the conference treasurer's office, there was not enough money to pay the bills.

The annual conference acted swiftly:

(1) It called on all churches to increase giving.

(2) It offered training in stewardship to pastors.

(3) It cut the budget, reducing staff and conference programs.

Problem solved! Right?

Wrong! The annual conference acted to deal with an immediate cash-flow problem. A deficit may not appear again for several years—if the conference is frugal and budgets conservatively.

But its problem is not solved. It will reappear, because nothing has been done to change or improve the system that produced the budget problem. In reality, the deeper problem has been covered over by reducing expenses.

Dealing with the real problem could prevent it from recurring. However, dealing with the real problem would be a major undertaking that would require:

- listening to the people in the congregations, understanding their reluctance to give, and determining what would bring them satisfaction and excitement in giving.
- providing occasions for people to witness and participate in opportunities for service beyond their own churches.
- understanding how some pastors are helping people open up new visions of faithfulness in loving their neighbors.
- removing barriers to people's motivation to extend the church.
- relating the quality of ministry people receive in their own churches to their openness to give and serve beyond the congregation.

Improving systems takes courage, leadership, and purposeful effort. Tampering with systems to remove the results of system ineffectiveness takes an ostrich and enough sand to properly bury its head.

I wish that kid would work on his system!

*March 1992*

## *Primary Task*

Week in and week out, Christian congregations interact with their communities. People leave the routine of daily living and enter into the gathered Christian community. When "church is over," they go back to the rest of their lives.

Sometimes people move into the Christian community and their lives are changed. They experience God anew. They glimpse new possibilities for living within and beyond the congregation. As they go back to live with family, friends, and strangers and to participate in the institutions of school, work, and play, they are different people—transformed by the mystical power of the Holy Spirit. They live differently; and the community and the world become more loving and just, because the people are move loving and just.

The fundamental community—church—community interaction is what we call the *primary task of the church*. It is not the only important transaction between community and congregation, but we believe it is essential and that it undergirds all other significant tasks of the congregation.

> *The fundamental community-church-community interaction is what we call the primary task of the church.*

The primary task of the Christian congregation is that weekly, repeatable cycle of reaching out to people who are burdened by persistent guilt and bringing them into the fellowship of the church, creating settings for them to experience the renewing power of God in their lives, nurturing them in the disciplines of Christian living, and then sending them out to live differently, as disciples of Christ who work for justice and love among all people.

That seems simple enough!

But it is not simple. It is less simple today than it was five years ago, and much less simple than twenty-five years ago. As our communities and societies become more diverse, more secular, more complex; as we increasingly think in individualistic terms; as we encounter radical discontinuities with the advent of each new generation; as the nature of family life, work, school, and health care has shifted; as the primary task of every basic social institution has become more obscure, so has the role of the church. Because it has become more difficult to understand and describe an institution's primary task, we have tended to ignore it, focusing instead on solving problems related to the institution.

However, problem solving does not improve the long-term functioning of an organization. Problem solving focuses on one small part of a system that has gone awry and seeks to bring it back to normalcy.

Something caused the problem to occur. It could have been a fluke or some extraordinary event caused by unknown outside intervention. If this is the first time the problem has occurred, we can fix it and go on. If it happens again, the system is malfunctioning. First, we fix the problem; then we immediately work on the system to repair what is causing the problem.

In 1965 the Methodist Church found that its vital signs were weak. We decided it must be a special cause, or that it just happened. The vital signs have been weak for more than twenty-eight years in a row!

We now have enough evidence to convince even the most stubborn among us that the system is not working well. We have worked on the problem. We have predicted a turnaround for the future. We have searched for the programs or methods that will improve our vital signs.

Now, it's time for us to work on the core system in each congregation and annual conference; to systematically repair the processes that are at the heart of any church's life...

- how people are received into the church;
- how they are related to God;
- how they are nurtured; and
- how they are sent out to serve.

Think for a moment about the primary task of a different kind of institution—a hospital. What is the core process or primary task of a hospital? It might be teaching. We need to teach people to be health-care specialists. When I'm sick, I want them to be there. It might be research—also very important. Hospitals can't improve their level of care unless they test new treatments and procedures. When I'm sick, I want the latest and the best.

It might be health care for people who are sick. This, we hope, *is* the hospital's primary task. If I'm in an automobile accident or become ill, I want to be taken to a hospital that defines its core process as receiving people who are sick or in pain, promptly testing for causes, acting with dispatch to treat the condition, and discharging patients as healthy people to live happy and productive lives. I want health-care providers to be well-trained, but I don't want to be taken to a hospital whose primary purpose is teaching. I want the latest and best treatment procedures, but I don't want to go to a hospital whose basic focus is research. I want to go where the core process is *health-care treatment.*

Churches, like hospitals, have many important tasks and processes. These might include child care, recreation for youth, acrobatics classes and handball games, and special programs for the elderly. Churches must give adequate attention to setting budgets, financing programs, building and maintaining facilities, and cooperating with other churches and community institutions.

*When I move to a new community or decide to visit a church for the first time, however, it is the functioning of the primary task that will attract or repel me.* The real issue when I want or need the church is: "Does this congregation reach out to me and pull me into a loving community, help me find God, stand by me, and then support me as I go out into the community?" The second issue is, "Is this process repeated with improved quality each week?"

The congregation may be small or large, rural or urban, denominational, or independent. The main consideration for anyone attending is the quality of the basic processes of entering, finding God, and living as a person intentionally following Christ.

Some churches are known for their organizational models. Some are known for their community programs. Some are known for the charismatic nature of their worship services. Others may specialize in youth ministry, singles' ministry, older adult ministry, mission outreach, having a diverse or interracial constituency, or an emphasis on doctrine.

The above-named ministries *contribute* to the core process. But the question I ask when I need help to make it through the week or when I feel estranged from God is, "Where is the church that has aligned *all* its processes to accomplish the primary task each week?"

If I were a pastor today, I would try to understand the community served by my congregation. I would ask, "Who in this community might be served by this congregation?" The congregation and I would then search for appropriate ways to reach the people in the community.

We would work on various means of creating settings for people to commune with God and be nurtured in the faith. We would follow up on in-church activities and have several ways of supporting people as they return home.

We would continue to work on the processes of coming in, seeking God, and going out until we found what worked most effectively. Then we would continually improve our methods and be on the lookout for new possibilities.

Why would I do these things as a pastor if I had the opportunity? Because they work. When I see vibrant churches that are reaching out to "all who have sinned and need a Savior" today, I find that these churches are successful because they focus on the basics—the primary task. Other, less successful churches look for the quick fix—the new evangelism program, the new stewardship gimmick, somebody else's formula for improving the Sunday school. For them, some things are in; others are out.

I'm in the church for the rest of my life. I want the basics and want to be part of the basics every week. Please don't offer me anything less.

*January 1993*

THINK ABOUT IT...

# Christian Community

Although there are many ways to state the task of the church (and no statement is necessarily better than another), the simple phrase *"faith development"* has long been efficacious for me. The phrase denotes the ongoing process of people who are working on the spiritual dimension of their lives and seeking God as the ground of their faith.

The phrase "faith development" indicates that ours is a journey by faith. Salvation is a gift of the grace of God. Our human search for God is incomplete, halting, and variously pursued. Our journey is based on an expectation, a hope, a perceived promise.

> *We are faithful disciples as we build Christian community in the church and as we take Christian community and build Christian community beyond the congregation.*

In recent days, I have been thinking about a complementary image of the task of the church; that is, the image of *"Christian community"* or *"building Christian community."* This image maintains the developmental, ongoing, growing, and improving aspect of the task of the church.

The United Methodist bishops in a pastoral letter last quadrennium talked about "Vital Congregations and Faithful Disciples." Their letter addressed how people live and act both as individuals and as members of a community. Vitality and faithfulness are addressed in relation to both the individual and to the Christian community.

It is easy for me to think of congregations as the means for producing disciples (the results). If congregations are the means and disciples are the ends or results, then we must ask: "How do we plan and act appropriately in the church to recruit, train, and turn out people with as many 'Christian' values or characteristics as possible?" From this view, those already in the congregation work to get others into the congregation and keep them there. We "fix " those who come and administer "managed spiritual health care" to maintain them as disciples.

There is another way to think about the church. Couldn't Christian community be seen as *an end as well as a process?* In this view, building Christian community and developing faithful disciples is essentially the same. Christian community is built in the congregation, but it is not wholly contained there. We don't see the congregation as the place we train people for doing something outside the church. We are faithful disciples as we build Christian community in the church and as we take Christian community and build Christian community beyond the congregation.

People come into the Christian community as seekers and pilgrims, joining with those who invited them. All are in the process together. Those who participate become leaders and mentors for others. There is no more "What should we do for them?" This view of the Christian community recognizes that we are all at different places in our search and stages of faith development.

### The Christian Community Is Different

Most people participate in some form of community—in the family, among friends, in work settings. These various communities sustain us, nurture us, and help us overcome loneliness, isolation, and selfishness. *The Christian community is different because it is built upon and revolves around Jesus, the Christ, rather than upon our mutual human needs alone.* It is a community focused on the God who gave us life, the God who redeems us in Christ, and the God who sustains us in the Spirit. It is a community in which we are attentive to God's work in the world, in our church, in us individually, and in all of us together.

*Christian community is more than people in communion with one another.* It is people together in communion with God through Christ, which provides a basis for our communion with one another. Faith development is living in Christian community. It begins as people are received by the community. It is deepened as people seek God, are found by God, and are transformed by God. It is nurtured as people worship, learn, and serve together. Faith development issues in faithful disciples as the Christian community moves out of the congregation into everyday life. Faithful disciples carry Christian community into all other communal relationships, so that even non-church communities can become Christian communities.

Christian community is inseparable from its results—faithful Christian disciples. Christian community is always…

| | | |
|---|---|---|
| Public | — | Never private |
| Inviting | — | Never limiting |
| Global | — | Never nationalistic |
| Open | — | Never closed |
| Cooperative | — | Never competitive |
| Giving | — | Never selfish |
| Removing barriers | — | Never building barriers |
| Inclusive | — | Never exclusive |

The Christian community is the body or community of Christ. It is people building knowledge about God and about the primary task of the congregation. It is people being received into a Christ-centered group, people being formed and nourished in Christ, and people taking Christian community into all their relationships.

I often encounter one of two views of the church: (1) the production work model, in which the church is producing disciples; or (2) the community model—people interacting with people (but not necessarily in a Christian community, in which people-to-people interactions are in the name, Spirit, and presence of Christ).

## Think About It...

*Our vision for The United Methodist Church in the General Board of Discipleship is that every United Methodist congregation be a **Christian community;** a force, an instigator, and a facilitator of faith development; a disciplined, active, and joyful body of Christ drawing people into Christian community and—through the power of Christ's indwelling Spirit—taking Christian community out to other people.*

To make this vision real, we must ask:

- How do people in congregations build competency for knowing God and one another?
- How do pastors and other professional leaders in the church build knowledge and competency for leading *Christian* congregations?
- How do these leaders help people build knowledge for living in Christian community?
- How do bishops and conference cabinets and leaders build knowledge to facilitate Christian community through disciplined attention to conference processes?

In addition, we need to consider these three questions:

- If pastors are not participating in *Christian* community, how can they facilitate Christian community in the congregations?
- In the United Methodist system, if pastors are not finding and participating in *Christian* community in and through the conference as a kind of "congregation of the clergy," where might they find it?
- If laypersons are not experiencing *Christian* community in their congregations…any suggestions?

*August 1993*

## More About Christian Community

Christian community is the essence of Christianity. Christian community is people seeking God through Christ and in the name of Christ. It is people praying for Christ to be present among them. Christian community is people studying the Scriptures to learn how God was present with people in biblical times and how God comes to us today in Christ.

Christian community is learning about Christ. It is studying the birth, life, and death of Jesus. It is pondering the testimony of the faithful first Christians who talked about his resurrection and ascension, his dwelling with us in the Spirit, and his oneness with God as the long-expected Messiah—the Christ. Christian community is learning to walk daily with Christ, to live fully and faithfully, to image Christ, to be examples of his compassion and justice, to be disciples and apostles, learners and teachers, seekers and prophets. Christian community is seeking God's will—through Christ—for Christians and for the whole world. It is praying—through Christ—for God's mercy when we fail or falter. It is asking for, hoping for, and believing in God's eternal salvation, so that in this world and in the world to come, we may live with God forever.

Christian community is people together with Christ. It is people together *with Christ.* And it is *people together* with Christ. Christian community is more than a *collection* of people seeking God through Christ; it is a *community.* It is people learning to live together in a special way—in Christ. Christian community is not a collective where the individual does not matter.

In Christian community, the individual and the group are made fully human and whole. The individual is transformed by the community into Christ-likeness. His or her life has integrity because it is connected to the One who gives life and to others who have been given life. In Christian community, the individual moves out of self, isolation, and private existence into openness to others, togetherness, and public life. In this movement, the individual becomes a whole person and—at the same time—a part of the whole body of Christ. Christ's church is the individual and the whole body—the community. The church is wherever the community is and wherever the individual is. The church extends as far as the parts of the body extend.

*The task of the Christian community is faith development.* At its deepest levels, the Christian community is a faith-building community. It is people in community seeking God and faith in God. It is people seeking to be faithful to one another and to support one another. Members of the Christian community build their faith together and live out that faith both communally and individually.

Unlike some communities, Christian community is never a closed community. Closure and exclusivity are not of the nature of Christ. Christian community is made up of people working together—in public—on their faith in Christ. Christian community is open, inviting, caring, and receptive of everyone.

## Think About It...

The Christian community is a *forming* and a *transforming* community. Through faith and the continuous development of faith in the cradling arms of the Christian community, people are changed by God. They become new creatures as they find the One they seek. The One they seek finds and receives them, and they are forever different.

As people's lives are redirected in the Christian community, the community celebrates and nurtures the awakening of the Spirit within them. Faith development continues as individuals and the whole community strive for spiritual maturity—a never-ending process.

Members of the Christian community live out their lives in all sorts of ways. One of those ways is within the Christian community itself. However, they also live as individuals and as family members. They work, play, and serve in places outside the gatherings of the Christian community. As members go from the gathered Christian community, they go to live as the Christian community, to build Christian community in other relationships, to tell others what they have experienced in the Christian community, and to invite others to experience Christian community themselves.

Christian communities are inviting, receptive, transforming, nurturing, and challenging. All these attributes together are the *core process of faith development*. Faith development is what Christian communities are, what they do, what they know how to do. Christian communities excel in faith development. Faith development is the primary task of the church. *All* aspects of that *primary task* or *core process* must be done. Christian communities always have done it, for, that is their very nature.

Christian faith development does not and can not take place consistently apart from the Christian community. The experience of humankind and the Christian church for two centuries makes that clear. Human community is a magnificent gift of God, but human community apart from the power and presence of Christ is not *Christian* community, and it cannot sustain Christian faith development. Christ is surely present in *all the world*—caring, beckoning, inviting. However, the pursuit of Christ individually is not sustainable. Individual pursuit of Christ is not of the nature of the God whom Christ came to reveal, the nature of God's creation, or the nature of Christ himself.

Christian community is people—through Christ—working on their faith together. Simply, the equation may be stated:

- You + I + Christ = Christian community.
- Christian community = faith development.
- Faith development = invitation + transformation + nurture + sharing and serving.

What if you experienced Christian community like that identified above, and then you lost it?

Who is holding the vision of the Christian community today?

What would it take to build Christian community anew in every United Methodist congregation?

*September 1993*

## Members and Customers

Jim Fenhagen is an Episcopal priest with the Cornerstone Project. In his newsletter, *A Cornerstone Reflection* (vol. 1, no. 1), he writes about "Leadership and Conflict":

> "'What really wears me down,' a young priest told me, 'is not the amount of work I do, but the climate of negativity in which my ministry takes place. Continuous back-biting and complaints about the church are as energy sapping as illness.' The pain of this priest tells us a lot about the state of today's church.
>
> The time has come for the Episcopal Church to begin building a climate of trust sufficient to deal with our differences without creating such negativity that leadership becomes more burden than joy."

> *Organizations that do not provide quality service and quality products do not survive.*

Jim Anderson, also an Episcopal priest and my long-time writing partner, engaged me in conversation about Fenhagen's interpretation of the young priest's dilemma. Upon reflection, we decided that a different view of the climate of negativity in many of our churches is appropriate (which Fenhagen has since acknowledged with gratitude).

\* \* \*

Jim (Anderson) and I suggest that this young priest and the members of the congregation whom the priest perceives as negative are operating out of two different frames of reference. We characterize these two orientations as a *membership frame of reference* (the orientation of the priest) and a *customer frame of reference* (the orientation of the laity).

Perhaps you have had the experience of dealing with a government bureaucracy—trying to get a license for your car perhaps—and of being frustrated by the lack of attention to your problem. Your frame of reference was that of a critical and unhappy customer who wanted personal attention, information that would clear your confusion, and timely service. The frame of reference of the government employee might be characterized as that of a person who is familiar with regulations, impatient with people who don't understand what is clearly written, and weary of repetitious complaints. Further, the employee is no doubt evaluated by the ability to follow procedure without exception.

One of the great changes that has occurred in American society over the last thirty years is sometimes called the *quality revolution*. For generations, Americans were willing to buy a Ford, GM, or Chrysler auto that wore out in three years and that often was a lemon. No more! The consumer movement is a reality. Organizations that do not provide quality service and quality products do not survive.

Who decides what is quality? The customer. In November 1993, *Fortune* magazine published a special Autumn/Winter issue entitled "The Tough New Customer." A statement from the managing editor, Marshall Loeb, in the issue is worth repeating:

> *"Sometimes a business trend is so powerful and pervasive that it demands far more attention than a single magazine can give it. When such a shift alters the most fundamental activities in all of commerce—buying and selling—then it's about as big as they come. That's just the sort of transformation that surrounds us and that prompts this special extra edition of <u>Fortune</u>."*

We believe that much of the research and commentary on the rise of individualism, the pervasive loss of loyalty to denominations and to employers, the movements to empower consumer interest groups, the loss of brand loyalty, the increased willingness to challenge the authority of leaders and institutions (Who thirty years ago would have been willing to question the authority of his or her physician?) is telling us that many church people are no longer loyal members of The United Methodist Church or Episcopal Church so much as they are customers or critical consumers who are seeking God and seeking someone who will listen and respond to the particular circumstances of their lives. We may lament this shift in people, but as *Fortune* magazine has indicated, the shift is most certainly a permanent one.

> *Many church people are no longer loyal members of The United Methodist Church or Episcopal Church so much as they are customers or critical consumers who are seeking God and seeking someone who will listen and respond to the particular circumstances of their lives.*

Even though the laity themselves do not always recognize the shift, the fact is that their frame of reference is no longer that of loyal members, willing to do what is asked, willing to subscribe to the authority of the priest or minister, willing to contribute as the price of belonging for the hope of a reward in the hereafter. Instead, each individual believes that he or she has the right and even the duty to make his or her needs known and, in many cases, to search for a setting that is going to provide a quality response to those needs. People often find, instead, an organization that—like many government agencies—simply cannot deal with people who demand service and who become impatient and critical when they don't get it. The clergyperson is like the lone, beleaguered clerk at the license bureau who is faced with a seemingly endless line of people seeking help, each of whom makes it to the front of the line irritated from the delay.

Trust, then, is not really the central issue. The issue is that we do not normally have a congregational system that is capable of responding to that long line of critical, individual seekers. In the hypothetical government office, is the climate of negativity an issue of trust between the harassed clerk and the citizens in line? Clearly no. The system, designed for a stable, docile population, is the culprit. The system—not the relationships among the key individuals—is what needs attention.

Trust becomes an issue only when relationships break down because the system does not facilitate people being heard and responded to on their terms. It is one thing to suggest that the clergy and laity need to work to build trust. It is another to offer the possibility of re-creating church systems to enable clergy to listen to laity at levels deep enough to understand that the role of people has shifted from members (owners) to consumers (responders).

\* \* \*

The issue before us is a difficult one. Few of us are prepared psychologically to accept the shift from *member to consumer.* We consider the issue a theological one. The word "member" goes with "church." The words "customer" and "consumer" go with business. We are not prepared for them to be used interchangeably.

We fail to struggle with the phenomenon, however, at our peril. The issue is particularly significant as we seek to serve the "Baby Boom" generation and their children. That's almost everyone under age 50. Laura Nash, in a *Christian Century* (January 5-12, 1994, p. 17) review of Wade Clark Roof's new book, *A Generation of Seekers*, points out that "Boomers' religious practices ... emphasize choice and personal experience. They shop churches, habitually switch brands, and consume religious products that reflect above all their own personal selfhood. America's religious center no longer holds."

It was that center that was made up of members.

*April 1994*

THINK ABOUT IT...

## *Evangelism*

I have been thinking a lot about evangelism lately. It seems particularly important to me as I try to pray more and orient my life more around other people. I am increasingly aware that Jesus really meant it when he said the first commandment is to love God and the second is to love neighbor—and that you do one when you do the other. As I become more needful of hearing and rehearing the story of God's love, I understand better that I need to tell that story myself more often.

I am discovering that evangelism is not something you learn to do. It is a state of being Christian—being part of the community gathered around Christ—his birth, life, death, resurrection—and Pentecost too. If you're a part of that community, you *do* evangelism. If you're not a part of that community, you don't. In other words, if one is not evangelical, he or she is on the fringe of Christian community at best. Martin Marty has said:

> "To evangelize is to meet people in situations where the Gospel of Jesus Christ is given the opportunity to change them, as individuals and groups, and to bring them toward wholeness—in other words, to 'save' them and to situate them in the context of Christian community, so that their lives will be enhanced and so that they can face together those questions of values, meanings, and service that also have eternal dimensions."

> *Evangelism is not something you learn to do. It is a state of being Christian–being part of the community gathered around Christ–his birth, life, death, resurrection–and Pentecost too.*

Most of us feel that The United Methodist Church is not very evangelical these days. Perhaps that means that we are not doing very well in developing Christian communities. Maybe we have communities, but not Christian communities. And maybe those human communities don't have the power to propel us "to meet people in situations where the Gospel of Jesus Christ is given the opportunity to change them."

In 1983, I wrote to 150 leaders of The United Methodist Church asking their thoughts about how the Discipleship Board could help them in their evangelism task. Responses from about one-half of them called for disseminating information about programs, methods, and resources. The following three suggestions were the most repeated responses:

(1) Locate the most effective programs in evangelism, interpret those programs, and share them with the whole church.
(2) Establish a centrally located United Methodist Training Center where people can be exposed to the best thinking, the latest methods, and

the finest instruction available. Include all things related to discipleship, but evangelism must be out front and primary.

(3) Provide resources for reaching special groups—the aged, singles, prisoners, handicapped persons, retarded adults, students, and others.

We have done our best to heed those prescriptions—Offering Christ Today Evangelism Schools, Growth Plus consultants, Vision 2000 events and training, New Life Missions and New World Missions, and special consultations on faith-sharing, church growth, and lay witnessing. Many of these efforts continue.

I am beginning to see evangelism in a different way. All the program building, method sharing, and resource development depends on the creation of Christian communities that are led by leaders who are learning how to grow in their own faith and are made up of people who are focused on God in Christ and are actively loving their neighbors—all of them. We keep trying to get our product right, yet we are neglecting the complete identification with people that Jesus modeled for us.

Evangelism *methods* have taken our attention from people—in community around Christ. We have grown lazy. We want someone else to learn how to do evangelism and then teach us. We measure church growth instead of meeting "people in situations where the Gospel of Jesus Christ is given the opportunity to change them."

In every congregation, there is a primary task that is either functioning or not functioning. If it is not functioning, evangelism is an empty word, Christian community is a distant theological concept, transformation gets defined as no change, and discipleship is impossible.

If the primary task is functioning, people are being reached out to and received in love, related to God, and nurtured in the Christian community; and they are meeting "people in situations where the Gospel of Jesus Christ is given the opportunity to change them." In these churches, people don't *talk* about evangelism. They work at building Christian community.

*May 1994*

THINK ABOUT IT...

# Wow! Was She Ever Wrong!

Five years ago, Alicia was appointed as pastor of Mt. Pleasant United Methodist Church, a church that has been in the community for a century. Although pastors have come and gone through the years, many of the church members have been at Mt. Pleasant for a long time.

Alicia assumed when she arrived on the scene that she would be the leader of the congregation. She planned to listen to the people, study the Scriptures, and manage the congregational system to help the people grow in their faith and discipleship.

*Wow! Was she ever wrong!* Five years of attempting to lead the congregation to change and improve has convinced Alicia that she is not the leader of the church. She is a pawn of the congregational system.

For several years, she blamed the church members. She thought they were sabotaging her efforts to be a good pastor. A wise counselor helped her see, however, that the church members are also at the mercy of the system. They did what the system trained them to do, what the system rewarded them for doing.

Alicia realizes now that it is inappropriate for a leader to blame the customers or the beneficiaries of an organization. Blaming those it serves is deadly for any organization. If such blaming continues, the organization will die.

Alicia's primary learning, however, is the power of an organizational system. The system can be like a sinister troll that controls what is acceptable or unacceptable. It is the guardian of past experiences and traditional values. It ensures conservation of the status quo.

> *The system...is the guardian of past experiences and traditional values...A firmly ensconced organizational system has the power to shield people from leaders who have the energy, vision, and desire to change things.*

A system, bolstered by the legitimization of age, is the repository of all that has been held sacred through the years. It judges, on behalf of all—the living and the dead—what will be permitted or rejected. The rationale for the rules of the system may have long since been lost, but the folk ways and mores serve as vital, unwritten rules about the conduct of participants.

An organizational system—apart from its leaders—does not have clear aim or mission. A system is pragmatic. Results are not understood or desired. The system values activity, vitality, enthusiasm, and celebration.

A firmly ensconced organizational system has the power to shield people from leaders who have the energy, vision, and desire to change things. A system that demands extensive program planning processes ensures that change will not happen. When a leader spends half of her energy persuading people to do "penance" by participating in priority setting enterprises and the other half of her energy performing the ceremonial functions of the organization, she does not have enough energy left to change things.

Alicia understands that she is not the real manager of the institution. Because she knows the manager is not another person, she can accept the situation. Further, Alicia is not defeated because she knows that the system can be re-created or reinvented. It can be taken apart and redesigned. It is never easy, but it is possible.

Alicia will need several more years of leadership in this church to succeed in the system change. The members of the church will have to share her desire for the new possibility. They need to begin with a new look at the church's mission and their own vision for their own community. They will then be able to form new processes into a system that will serve the church's mission and permit the people to make it real in their community.

*Wow! Was she ever wrong!* Indeed, Alicia was wrong in the beginning. She blamed the congregation, even as they blamed her and her predecessors for what was, in reality, a system problem. The system was wrong. What Alicia and the congregation have to figure out is how to make the system right.

*June 1994*

## Marketing the Church

The church is people together in the presence of Christ. The church is people seeking God through Christ, being transformed through the grace of God's atonement in Christ, and learning to live as loving and faithful disciples of the one who came from God.

The church is more. It is people sharing what they have seen and heard with others. There is urgency in communicating this good news. It is so good that it can't be contained or saved within the church.

As Christians, telling others what we see and hear is not easy in our day (or in any day, for that matter). Telling the good news is much more difficult than telling about a new car or the comfortable fit of a certain brand of shoes. Telling others about God's love and redemption that reconciles us to one another and to God simply is more difficult to weave into a conversation. The issue doesn't come up in everyday conversation, and it is sometimes difficult to introduce the subject without awkwardness.

Further, some of us find that we are not very good at talking about spiritual matters. Some are better at living their faith than they are at talking about it. They follow St. Francis's dictum: "Preach the Gospel; if necessary, use words."

In addition, what seems to get the attention of some people becomes a barrier for others. Therefore, the ever-important issue of the church is the evangelical question: How do we share the gospel so that it is received in a way that takes hold of the hearer and leads to his or her transformation by God?

The evangelical issues involving communication and relevancy are similar to marketing issues in the business world. But one form of marketing is inappropriate for the church (and—I believe—inappropriate for any organization). I am referring to marketing that begins with a service or product and seeks to create customers for it. The marketer attempts to position the service or product so that people will believe they need it, whether they do or not. That form of marketing manipulates people. It treats people as a profit source, and it measures success in dollars rather than in improved quality of life for people.

An appropriate form of communicating is person-centered. It recognizes the diversity of people and notes the differences in their abilities to hear and respond to what is offered. It is this kind of sharing that the church wants to engage in with the world around it.

This form of "marketing" begins with listening to people to understand

> *An appropriate form of communicating is person-centered. It recognizes the diversity of people and notes the differences in their abilities to hear and respond to what is offered.*

their needs and receptivity and to determine the appropriate "language" for communicating with them. It honors people's hurts, hopes, and yearnings for God, and it seeks to respond appropriately. Listening must go beneath the surface, for listening is not intended to find a "hook" to manipulate people. Rather, listening is done with deep levels of love and compassion so that the listener comes to know the songs in the hearts of the people. As we, the listeners, hear people's songs, we are able to sing those songs back to them when their memories fail. We are also able to sing them a new song—a song of the Spirit—if that is what they seek.

Further, listening to people to understand and invite them into a grace-filled relationship with God in Christ is listening for God in the very people we seek to relate to God. Listening is believing in and seeking God's prevenient grace that goes before and prepares the way for God's transformation.

\* \* \*

If we in the church listen carefully to people in the world around us in our day, we hear people differing fundamentally in the way they relate to organizations and primary social institutions.

Demographic studies conducted since mid-century have shown that people born before 1950 tend to have a "membership-orientation." They are joiners and belongers who are loyal and obedient to group norms. People born after mid-century, however, tend to have a "customer-orientation." Seeking that which fulfills the "self," they often change tastes and loyalties. They tend to be highly individualistic. Of course, some people of both orientations are members of all generations, and people differ in scores of other attributes too.

What the church needs to know is that the wholesale condemnation of "marketing" in the church (defined as telling our story and inviting people to respond to God's marvelous grace by better listening to and understanding people) is as disastrous for the church as engaging in manipulative marketing practices. Both extremes deny the evangelical urgency of the Christian gospel and the relentless pursuit of Jesus.

Peter Francese, president of *American Demographics,* writing about elections in the United States in an editorial in that magazine (November 1994, p. 2), concluded by saying, "Perhaps we should quit trying to change people's minds with data and spend more time asking them what is on their minds. Who knows? We might uncover some real issues and real problems..."

If we in the church spent more time listening to people, we might discover some ways of being the church and extending the church that go well beyond our present experience.

*January 1995*

THINK ABOUT IT...

## Let's Not Turn the Message Into Bait

Recently, while leading a Quest for Quality Seminar for two hundred pastors, I presented the heart of the Quest perspective on the church's primary task, which is:

(1) reaching out and receiving all who will come,
(2) creating settings in which people can seek God and be transformed by God,
(3) nurturing people in Christian discipleship,
(4) and sending them out to build a loving and just world.

I spent a good deal of time demonstrating that the primary task is one continuous process of people being transformed into disciples. I explained that the process cannot be broken into parts (even these four parts) for programming. The only way to improve one part of the process is to work on all the parts.

A seminar participant responded that evangelism (which he interpreted to be "reaching out and receiving all who come") was important in its own right and should be pursued—even if the church does not have a system in place for the rest of the process.

My response was direct and unequivocal. "I disagree," I said. "Don't invite me into your church if you don't have the ability to put me all the way through. I don't want to get invited in and get lost looking for what's next. If you can't provide settings for me to listen and respond to God and to prepare me for a life of following Jesus, then don't bother me."

The participant's retort was, "We have to trust God and have faith that God will change us whether we are set up for that or not."

> ❧ *Are we creating settings that will include all who will come? Are we creating settings for seeking God and letting God change us? And are we creating settings that open us to be responsive to God's launching us into the world?"*

What do you think? Am I faithless person who is pursuing works righteousness? Is the man with whom I spoke faith-filled and radically trusting God?

Upon arriving home from the seminar, I found in the mail a printed sermon from Marianne Niesen, co-pastor of St. Paul's United Methodist Church in Helena, Montana. She had preached on February 5, 1995, on the lectionary reading from the Gospel of Luke (5:1-11) regarding Jesus' directions to the disciples concerning catching fish. ("Put out into the deep water and let down your nets for a catch...Do not be afraid; from now on you will be catching people.") The Rev. Niesen writes:

> "We join the groups that have not just a message, but a place for us.
>
> "We join the groups that listen to what we need and receive what we bring and call out what we can become in God's eyes. That's what church is meant to do.
>
> "If you think I sound somewhat frustrated with traditional Christian evangelism—I am. I think we've done tremendous damage to the message of Jesus. We've made it into bait we throw at people rather than a life to live."

I agree with her position. We don't, through our rituals, cause God to come and save us. God is alive in the world today, working miracles and extending grace. We cannot cause it, and we cannot stop it. Hallelujah! Praise God! (If people could have stopped God's action in the world, they would have done so long ago.)

The issue is not what God is doing through the living Christ among us, but whether or not we United Methodists (congregations and people) are watching expectantly and listening with our hearts. We need to ask, "Are we creating settings that will include all who will come? Are we creating settings for seeking God and letting God change us? And are we creating settings that open us to be responsive to God's launching us into the world?"

*June 1995*

THINK ABOUT IT...

## Confusion About the Journey

The world is on a spiritual quest, while the church is on an activity quest. That may seem to be a harsh observation, but look at your congregation to see if it is true.

We have a choice: We can work directly on what needs to work in the church for the church to be the church—namely, the spiritual disciplines—or we can work on activities that either substitute for the spiritual disciplines or (supposedly) help us plan to practice the disciplines.

In her book, *Peripheral Visions,* Mary Catherine Bateson writes, "Children who are given chocolate milk to get calcium into them grow up as chocolate eaters, not as milk drinkers" (page 112). If the church puts people on a diet of activity (serving on committees and putting together plans for ministry) rather than helping people learn how to pray, study the Scriptures, and pursue the means of grace, the church may find that it has produced an organization of good activities rather than Christian community and people seeking God and being transformed by God.

> *The world is on a spiritual quest, while the church is on an activity quest ... What needs to work in the church are settings where people can seek God instead of activities that help people plan for seeking God.*

What needs to work in the church are settings where people can seek God instead of activities that help people plan for seeking God. The future of the General Board of Discipleship is in resourcing the church to help people do this. The future of our whole church depends on our creating these settings. The value in this board is in helping the church create arenas for seeking God, practicing the spiritual disciplines, and working on faith development.

Much that we have been doing in the General Board of Discipleship has prepared us for this task, but we cannot continue the programming activity model that we perfected in the past. We will continue to value and to build competencies in skill areas. All our staff will build knowledge in several areas. However, our vision has changed. Instead of heeding the advice, "Don't just sit there, do something," we are learning to value the idea that "when you don't know what to do, just sit there—and listen."

We are seeking to help the church build knowledge of three types:

(1) Mystical, spiritual knowledge of God.

(2) Knowledge of the church (which mediates knowledge of God).

(3) Knowledge for improvement of church processes; or how to be spiritual leaders and Christian disciples within the church and beyond the church in all the world.

Our role is to learn with those we serve to help them build knowledge—in appropriate combinations—in these three areas.

The world is on a spiritual quest; our church is on a creative activity quest. We recently announced a new growth process dealing with spirituality that had space for forty people. More than 700 people applied.

The church cannot compete with the secular world in activity. Further, we cannot simply become more creative in our activities. At the General Board of Discipleship, we are moving from programming functions to undergirding churches that are helping people approach God with a listening heart. At first glance, the differences may seem subtle, but the change is radical.

- It is not our task to help pastors learn to preach. We will help them learn how to state and hold the vision of people seeking God and God seeking them.
- It is not our task to strengthen the Sunday school. We will help churches create small groups of many kinds for practicing and living the faith.
- It is not our task to provide tested worship liturgies. We will help pastors help people seek and celebrate God's continuing miracles of grace.
- It is not our task to teach people to be generous givers. We will help people respond lovingly to God's gifts.
- It is not our task to teach anything. We will help people learn out of their need to grow faithfully.
- It is not our task to motivate people to do something. We will help people remove the barriers to responding graciously to God's mercy.
- It is not our task to help people be more active in the church. We will help people spend as little time in the church as possible and more time living in the world as loving disciples.
- It is not our task to teach methods of evangelism. We will help congregations create systems that can run only on high-test evangelical witnessing.
- It is not our task to help churches offer programs for families. We will help congregations shift the primary responsibility for spiritual growth back to the family and help the family learn to build Christian community.
- It is not our task to entertain or inspire men with creative programs. We will help the church invite men to salvation and sanctification.

Nothing is scared that is not sacred. We will push beyond attending to resources and activities to identifying with those we serve. What people need to be the church and to lead the church will be our motivation as a board.

I invite you to compare the two lists below.

## Think About It...

| Church Work Areas | Wesley's Means of Grace |
|---|---|
| Missions | Doing no Harm |
| Church and Society | Study of the Word |
| Evangelism | Prayer |
| Education | The Lord's Supper |
| Worship | Fasting |
| Stewardship | Spiritual Conferencing |
| | Acts of Mercy |

The world is on a spiritual quest. The church is on an activity quest. The great Methodist layman and ecumenist John R. Mott saw the difference a half century ago:

> *"An alarming weakness among Christians is that we are producing Christian activities faster than we are producing Christian experience and Christian faith; that the disciplines of our souls and the deepening of our acquaintance with God are not proving sufficiently thorough to enable us to meet the unprecedented expansion of opportunity and responsibility of our generation."*

*September 1995*

## A New Quest? Let's Focus On Essentials

***Do you believe that God is alive today – that the record of God's presence and activity in the world is being written today, even as it was in biblical times?*** Failing to believe in God's continuing activity can lead to a hardened or fundamentalist position about what it means to be Christian. Such a position says, "I have the truth" instead of "I am seeking the truth."

***Do you believe that the living God is present in all the world – not just in the church?*** Failing to believe that God is present *in the world* can lead to false and devastating dichotomies between the church and the rest of the world.

***Do you believe that the church is Christian community – not just community, but people in community with Christ at the center?*** The church lives its life as hospitable, Christ-centered, people-focused people who become the means of grace for one another and – with one another – become channels of grace to the world. We enter Christian community as individuals, asking what the church can do for us. We continue as part of the church, asking how we can be fully participating, loving members of the company of believers. Our failure to do so could lead us to conclude that being in any pleasing group is the same as being the church.

***Do you believe that we seek God through obedience to the first and second commandments of Jesus Christ?*** Historically, the church has sought God as it has gathered regularly for worship, faithfully practicing the spiritual disciplines of prayer, Bible study, the Lord's Supper, fasting, acts of service, and the like. It has sought God as it has listened with a loving heart to all the people of the world. Failing to participate in the gathered body can lead persons to try to be Christian disciples apart from the Christian community or to try to love God without loving other people.

***Do you believe that the task of the church is transformation?*** When the church focuses on people and the world, it is an agent of the world's transformation through the power of the gospel. Failing to focus on people and the world can lead the church to turn its focus on itself and thus become powerless.

***Do you believe that the church is missional – living to give its life away – because of the character of the one who called the church into being?*** The church is not merely "doing good" when it is missional and evangelical; it is being the church – fulfilling its purpose. Failing to be missional and evangelical can lead us to think, " But we need the money here at home."

***Do you believe that God calls and sends leaders as means of grace for the people?*** Leaders in the church are often categorized as lay, consecrated, or ordained. In the world, they are all simply leaders or disciples or servants. The categories differ in the nature of the call and the sending – not in rank or privilege. Their accountability is to God and to one another. Failing to be accountable or to remember the servant nature of leadership can lead to "professionalized" clergy and an elitist caste system in the church.

In each time and place, the church recalls and rehearses its mission, listens anew to God and to people to understand people's deepest yearnings, and re-images its vision for the Christian community and its work of faithful discipleship. Making mistakes and learning as it goes along (and sometimes starting over), the church molds itself around its vision and moves out. Each day, the processes and systems of the church are molded and remolded, and proved and improved around the vision.

The church continually asks how to seek God, listen to God, and love God; how to seek people, listen to people, and love people.

Rather than focusing on the institutional church, we focus on people and the work of the church and how they intersect. Rather than asking God to bless our church and our efforts to build and improve the church, we seek to be and build the church where we encounter God and find evidence of God's blessings.

## *Appropriate Systems Are Needed*

Appropriate systems for supporting and undergirding Christian community are necessary for the church to be the church and to continue as the church. As the vision changes, the systems must also change and improve. We have delayed the task of putting appropriate systems in place for The United Methodist Church of the present day. We must now give attention to that task. God works miracles in our churches every day and blesses us and uses us even in our brokenness. But we can improve in our response and faithfulness.

Even a cursory survey of the processes of The United Methodist Church today reveals results that are antithetical to our vision, our values, our expectations for the Christian community, and our hopes for inclusion and eternal participation in God's reign.

In an ideal world, a world of linear, orderly processes, we begin with a vision, construct worldly structures and processes as supports for moving toward the vision, and continuously change and improve the system of structures and processes as we extend the vision and as we learn and build knowledge for improvement. We watch for leaders – people whom God calls forth – to facilitate our developing faithfulness. Our leaders help us clarify our common vision so that we can be centered on Christ, who gives us the vision. We become a traveling people – pilgrims and seekers – going where we are sent and extending the Christian community.

United Methodists today, however, do not and cannot live in an ideal world. We are a broken people. Our world is not orderly, and our processes are not linear. Our condition is hopelessness, fear, mistrust, division, suspicion, and dejection.

We do not have the option of starting over. We cannot begin from nothing. Hundreds of years of accumulated structures and processes hold our loyalties and exhaust our energies. Some structures and processes work well, some poorly, and some not at all. The system resulting from the combination is frightfully inadequate. It does not allow us to be a movement people. It anchors us in the past and causes us to use our energy to disentangle ourselves rather than to encourage our seeking God and God's new vision every day.

Could we change? Could we disentangle ourselves? Could we venture forth on a new quest? Could we give it all up – give up all the accouterments of being church as we know it? Could we simplify our church lives and take from our institutions – past and present – only what is absolutely necessary to be the church – a little bread and wine for focusing on Christ and a towel and a little water for being servant disciples?

What more do we really need in the church than transcendent worship and small bands of the Christian community traveling together as missionary servants?

Could we simplify, focus on essentials, love one another, and refuse to be sidetracked by all that now divides and destroys us?

The good news – and perhaps the only news we need – is that God in Christ is alive and moving among us – even today – in all the world. The story of the church is a new story that is being written at this moment. As members of the Christian community, we focus on loving God and neighbor, which means we travel as missionaries, evangelists, and agents of God's continuing transformation of people and the world.

*November 1995*

THINK ABOUT IT...

> *"Quality improvement is important in these times…to help us shift our focus as The United Methodist Church from institutional maintenance to a focus on the people and our communities and their needs."*
>
> *—Sharon Brown Christopher*
> *Bishop, Minnesota area*

# CHAPTER 3:

## QUALITY IMPROVEMENT AND CHANGE

Quality Is Guaranteed ..................................................................62
The New and the Old ..................................................................63
When the Revolution Comes, Everything Changes ............................65
Building Knowledge....................................................................68
Satisfaction Guaranteed................................................................70
Getting It Backward ....................................................................72
A Bishop Responds to Concerns About Quality Improvement.............73
Moments of Truth .......................................................................76
Always Another Call ...................................................................78

THINK ABOUT IT...

## *Quality Is Guaranteed*

A customer bought a new car—a Saturn, the automobile made by General Motors; but the car began to give her trouble. When she returned it to the Saturn dealership, she was told that she would be given a new car to replace her malfunctioning one.

About five years ago, Saturn gave new cars to 1,836 customers because their cars had been damaged by a corrosive coolant in the engine cooling system. "The cars can be repaired, but we're saying, 'Bring the car in and we'll give you a new, comparable car,'" said Bill Betts, a spokesman for Saturn.

"We'll put them [owners] in rental cars until their cars come in," said Roger Rains, the general manager of a Saturn dealership. *Quality is guaranteed.*

Another customer went to a fast-food restaurant to buy dinner for his family. The wait seemed unusually long, but the customer did not complain. However, when the manager realized how long the man had been waiting, she returned his money and gave him the food at no cost. The manager indicated that the service the restaurant had given did not meet its own expectations. *Quality is guaranteed.*

A group of people entered a large full-service restaurant and were seated in a section where no server had been assigned. When they realized they were not going to be served, the customers got the attention of the manager, who exclaimed: "Oh no! This meal is on me, and I insist that you have dessert. We do not have this part of the restaurant open this evening. You should not have been seated here." *Quality is guaranteed.*

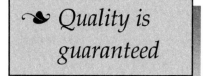

That same group of people visited the local United Methodist church. They attended as active seekers, hoping to find God, to be inspired, to find hope.

The worship service they attended was not bad. It was more boring and irrelevant than bad. The sermon was hollow, even though the pastor seemed to be a nice person. The people were friendly—but lifeless. The "customers" did not find much at the church to inspire them or to encourage them to return.

The leaders of The United Methodist Church responded...

*August 1991*

## The New and the Old

In 1991, Wal-Mart was our nation's largest retailer. At about the same time, Kmart was the second largest. Sears, which had been the largest retail company for many years, was third.

"...Its [Sears] ossified organization has made it less able to sell at a competitive price and a profit," wrote Bill Saporito in the May 6, 1991, issue of *Fortune* magazine (pages 50-59). The writer anticipated a dogfight between Wal-Mart and Kmart as they competed with each other in many communities. He considered Target a third contender.

All three of the combatants (Wal-Mart, Kmart, and Target) for the top retailing position began operating in 1962. The *Fortune* article noted that the top ten discount retailers in 1962 are no longer in existence.

> *Institutions do not last forever. They rise in response to a need or an opportunity and may flourish for a time—maybe for a long time.*

Institutions do not last forever. They rise in response to a need or an opportunity and may flourish for a time—maybe for a long time. Then the world changes, and other institutions are born. Their time in the limelight will also be limited by changes around them and by their ability to adapt to those changes.

Some institutions are able to adapt. They are able to change and survive because they pay attention to the changing needs and desires of the people they serve. They remove barriers between leaders and people. They are led by people who are clear about the organization's mission and purpose. Their leaders know what business they are in and strive to be the best. They make learning, which guides change, important for everyone.

Successful institutions are constantly searching for new markets, new services, new programs, and new products. They close nonproducing or low-producing installations and open new ones in new places. The new ones may flourish because the new settings are more hospitable, or because the new outlets are not tied to outdated ways of operating.

The United Methodist Church has not created new congregations—except spasmodically—for a third of a century. We have, therefore, not adapted to a changing world. We are like those retailers that flourished in the middle of the century and are now dead or dying. We are stuck on saving the congregations we have, many of which are dying. Witness the extensive pattern of church subsidies in every annual conference of The United Methodist Church. Look at the character of some of the churches we are trying to prop up.

A few voices keep calling for more new churches. There is no question that establishing new churches is the ultimate necessity. However, let's face the facts. Our current system does not allow us to start new congregations.

Our system does not have the capacity for starting new congregations as long as so many resources go toward propping up large numbers of existing congregations.

Some subsidized churches clearly are missional and deserve our support. Others need to be supported locally, fitting programs to available resources. How can we tell the difference?

Churches in areas of extreme poverty, churches serving people devastated by catastrophe, churches serving communities where there are not other Christian churches, and churches in communities expected to experience significant population growth may need to receive short-term or temporary subsidies. The denomination as a whole has a stake and an opportunity in such churches.

> *What if we redesigned our system to look to the future, to focus on new ministries in new places, to reach out rather than to turn inward to prop up the past?*

What if we redesigned our system to look to the future, to focus on new ministries in new places, to reach out rather than to turn inward to prop up the past?

Under a redesigned system, churches that have not been able to change with their communities would die. Churches that adapt to change would find new life as they joyfully participate in starting new congregations. New congregations would open possibilities for ministry that today we cannot even imagine—in urban and rural areas, among all social classes, with countless immigrant groups, in all types of communities. Some congregations would be started in communities where other United Methodist congregations had served other constituencies in other times.

Our future is not uncertain. We know what we can do to continue the ministry of The United Methodist Church as long as God chooses to use us. We also know the likely results of our present course of action. What is uncertain is whether we will give up a system designed to preserve the past in order to redesign the system to build a new church for the future.

The system can be redesigned! Why don't we do that? The results we get would then be the results we want.

*October 1991*

# When the Revolution Comes, Everything Changes

Organizations in the United States and around the world that are producing quality goods and services are those that have built systems that are capable of continuous improvement. Quality organizations listen to their customers, set their aim *beyond* the highest expectations of their customers, and continuously improve their systems to provide higher levels of quality. Their customers do not know all that is happening, but they do know that they are continually surprised and delighted.

Does the path to quality in the church begin with a quiet strategy of improving basic processes in the organization (whether it be the congregation, annual conference, or general church) or with a revolution? The strategies in organizations outside the church are mixed. Moreover, what is considered quiet, strategic change to some may seem revolutionary to others. The view of change depends in part on where a person stands in relation to the organization. Radical change in the church will affect clergy and laity differently.

> *Does the path to quality in the church begin with a quiet strategy of improving basic processes in the organization...or with a revolution?*

The nature and explosiveness of the change necessary to turn an organization around is primarily related to the organization's present system. Is the present system capable of improvement, of basic change? Any organization is capable of cosmetic changes, but some organizations may not be capable of fundamental change.

When Ford and General Motors got serious about competing with Japanese and European auto makers, each company chose different strategies. Ford worked quietly to build and improve the *Taurus*, which has been a success in the marketplace. General Motors built a state-of-the-art plant in Tennessee and developed the *Saturn*, which is also selling well.

Some systems deteriorate over time, and it is best to destroy the old system and build a new one. The United States Postal Service may be one of them. Private companies have become so effective in delivering packages and letters that the United States Postal Service may have lost the ability to compete. However, with the right leadership, the postal service might regain its former strength.

Most United Methodists would agree that The United Methodist Church system is not working well today. It does not produce the high quality results we want. The system once worked to produce quality. That is why, in its early history, it became the largest, most widely dispersed Protestant church.

No one plotted to destroy The United Methodist Church, but for more than a hundred years, the church's organizational system has been bombarded by the forces of change in our society. In some ways, the system could not adjust appropriately. In other ways, it was forced to adjust inappropriately. The church has taken legislative actions that must be rescinded to rebuild the system fully. Even more important, the informal norms and habits of The United Methodist Church move us away from the actions we need to take to improve the system. For example, instead of withdrawing into our congregations, we need to improve conference processes. Instead of lobbying for votes for our special causes, we should be discussing our visions for the church and society that could prompt new action. Some of the myths and stories we tell one another are paralyzing. The present system can be rebuilt for a different future, but that new system should continue to be based on the Wesleyan foundations of...

> *The one ingredient common to all revolutions, whether violent or quiet, is leaders who can state the vision, design and build a system to carry out the vision, and manage the system to produce the results that people want.*

- Scriptural holiness
- Flexibility
- Discipline
- Continuous improvement
- Intrinsic and thoroughgoing connectionalism.

The task before us is like constructing a new jail using the bricks of the old jail without losing any prisoners. Change is difficult. Everything we do affects everything else, and we can't change everything at the same time.

We know that ministry is taking place in many United Methodist churches, and we don't want to lose any ground. It is safer to hold what we have and try some creative ideas to put a new face on our old body. That is precisely what we have been doing, and that is why we do not get different results.

Talk as we might about starting over or building a different system, that is not possible for United Methodists. We are connectional people, organized in annual conferences. Each annual conference is capable of rebuilding and improving its system of providing leaders for its congregations. Appropriate leadership in congregations can reestablish the church's primary task of...

- reaching out and receiving people into the loving fellowship of the church;
- relating people to God in Christ;
- nurturing and supporting people in the Christian faith;
- sending people to live as faithful disciples in the world.

When the primary task is functioning in every congregation of an annual conference, it can be continually improved. Conferences that learn how to have the primary task functioning in every congregation will inspire and help other conferences.

We are talking about revolution—even if it does not begin with a cataclysmic event. Other revolutions—the civil rights movement, the women's movement, and the liberation of Eastern Europe—sprang from seeds sown earlier. The one ingredient common to all revolutions, whether violent or quiet, is leaders who can state the vision (which is embedded in the hearts of people), design and build a system to carry out the vision, and manage the system to produce the results that people want.

Many of the people in leadership positions in The United Methodist Church are not truly leading. Rather, they are trying to manage the present system in new ways to produce different outcomes. The outcomes do not change because the present system is not designed to produce the results we want.

A few people in strategic leadership positions *are* able to envision a different system that is built upon new visions of the people. They envision a system that is designed for results related to faith development, seeking and finding God, spiritual discernment and formation, and neighborly caring. The new system as envisioned is constructed not only with knowledge and understandings about theology, Scripture, and religious rituals, but also with knowledge about people, organizations, change, motivation, and human behavior.

These church leaders are committed to patience, discipline, and long-term improvement in order to make the transition from the old to the new. They understand that the change they seek is so extensive that they too must change. They are willing to change the way they think, lead, and act; and they are secure enough to model those changes for all to see. They are wise enough to understand that as others see change in their leaders, they too are willing to change.

Finally, the leaders who are becoming agents of change in the church are wise enough to comprehend that whether the transition begins with fireworks or quiet prayer, it is a revolution. It is a revolution of the same magnitude as that launched by the Wesleys. These leaders know that when the revolution comes, everything changes! Everything!

*May 1993*

## Building Knowledge

What else could we possibly do to improve our United Methodist ministry? We've tried almost everything. We have preached, cajoled, cried, blamed, given prizes, set priorities, prayed, studied, searched the Scriptures, rethought our theology, argued, voted, negotiated, issued manifestoes and declarations, thought new thoughts, and tried to be creative.

We must find other ways to think about the church and its ministry, new ways to frame questions, and new ways to approach the improvement of our system.

Our present system appears tired, bereft of nourishment and energy, a relic of better days, incapable of improvement without radical redesign and differently motivated and trained leaders. If our present system cannot deliver the results we want, perhaps we need to ask, "How can we increase the capacity of our church for improvement?" This question is different from "What's wrong and how do we fix it?" When we have a system that is not working well *and* that rejects improvement, we must consider how we can intervene and change the system's capacity for improvement.

*If we ignore the possibility that our present system may be incapable of improvement, we may be forever doomed to trying to fix an unfixable system.*

How do we make entry into our system, not to fix it, but to increase its capacity to be improved? The answer to this question is related to the concept of building knowledge for improvement.

We build knowledge all the time. We build knowledge for living in society, for the roles we fill in life. We build knowledge for riding a bicycle, driving a car, or getting to work in the most efficient way amid changing conditions. A doctor builds knowledge, not just about medicine, but about how to facilitate healing—a much more difficult assignment.

Building knowledge is more than acquiring skills or information. It is moving from data gathering to understanding, from being informed and knowledgeable to being competent and wise. Methods for building knowledge move us along the path from questions to surveys, insights, hunches, hypotheses, and theories, to integration, and then to simple competence, discernment, and artful competence.

Building knowledge is a process of continually improving our ability to operate in a particular setting or culture. *Building knowledge* for improvement emphasizes the inadequacy of maintaining the status quo in our fast-changing society.

In the church, we need to build knowledge (1) of God; (2) of the Christian life; (3) of faithful discipleship; (4) of servant ministry; (5) of Christian community. Some of us need knowledge for leading congregations and for leading conferences and agencies that resource and support congregations.

Not everyone in the church needs to build the same knowledge. All of us need to build knowledge in the first five categories above, but even that knowledge is built differently for different people. Knowledge building for pastors is different from knowledge building for laity. Conference and general church leaders build knowledge in still other contexts and ways.

How can we increase the capacity of the congregation to help people build knowledge of God, of Christian community, and of Christian living so that they may continue to build knowledge of Christ and Christian community wherever

## Chapter 3: Quality Improvement and Change

they go?

A central issue is the ability of the pastor as congregational leader to build knowledge for leadership. Also at issue is how the church system enables that leader to improve his or her capacity for leading so that others are helped to improve congregational processes of faith development.

For many people in a congregation, building knowledge of God is enough. Others need to build knowledge about teaching, presiding, singing, or serving. Pastors, in addition to building knowledge of God, need competency in listening, leading worship, staffing, and group dynamics. Each role in the system needs knowledgeable people who can improve their capacity for building knowledge for further improvement.

United Methodist pastors have been exposed to valuable information about God, the church, church history, our Wesleyan tradition, preaching, the Bible, counseling, and much more in our seminaries. Most have also learned about human nature and related disciplines. We must ask, however, how many of us have built knowledge in helping the laity to build knowledge about God and faithfulness to God in human relationships?

Many pastors have focused on learning to do ministry themselves, rather than on helping the laity build knowledge to do ministry. Some may not have built knowledge at all. They learned what to do from experience and they keep doing it, even when the situation calls for them to do something different. Some of us with thirty years experience really have one year of experience that we have repeated thirty times.

We should not blame our pastors. The conferences of our church have failed us. They have turned the core process of the annual conference—recruiting, testing, training, providing credentials, and deploying congregational leaders—over to one or two committees and have turned their attention to lesser things. Conference leaders have done far too little thinking about the areas in which pastors need to build knowledge. They have assumed that graduation from seminary is a measure of knowledge and that exposure to selected information is adequate for congregational leadership.

*Lack of information is not the problem in our church. Lack of competency—the ability to build knowledge to the point of ready and adequate use in complex contexts—is the problem.* Some of us have built that competency in some of our appointments, but not in others. Some have never done it; and some always do it. Those who have built such competency have done so, in many cases, without the help of the conference system.

Somehow, we have to increase our capacity for improving our church systems. I believe the concept of building knowledge for improvement by people who approach the task from differing roles...

- the people in the community
- the people in the pews
- teachers and leaders
- pastors and diaconal ministers
- bishops and superintendents
- general church leaders

...is a good place to start.

*June 1993*

THINK ABOUT IT...

## Satisfaction Guaranteed

The card below was on the desk in the room when I checked in recently at a Hampton Inn.*

I paid. My stay at Hampton Inn was and always is a quality experience. Because of the moderate cost, efficient service, and customer orientation, I stay there often. I used to stay regularly at Holiday Inn, Ramada Inn, Howard Johnson, and the like; but many of those well-known, older hotel chains haven't realized that a quality revolution has occurred.

Some of our United Methodist churches haven't realized it either. Quality improvement has indeed happened in the church, but the changes are primarily outside the mainline. There is almost a direct parallel in churches' and hotels' ability to attract and hold people. Those that used to do it best have lost the ability to lead the rest.

I have been thinking about a card that could be included in the Sunday bulletin in United Methodist churches—maybe something like the one below:

*Hampton Inn Trademark used by permission.*

Maybe the guarantee would say:

> We guarantee
> our members are worn out,
> there is lots of work to do,
> and we will put you to work immediately.

*—or—*

> We guarantee
> we will take you in, shape you up,
> and ship you out in
> better shape then we got you.

*—or—*

> We guarantee
> friendly people, a caring fellowship, and
> good preaching (if the bishop sends us a good preacher).

*—or—*

> We guarantee
> a warm and accepting Christian community
> that will help you in your search for God,
> nurture you in the faith,
> teach you the Scriptures,
> enroll you in the whole ministry of the people of God,
> and send you out to live as Christ's disciple.

I need some help on this one. How would you state the guarantee? It needs to be related to who we are as Christ's people, what we do, what people are seeking from the church, and how we understand God is moving among us.

*October 1993*

THINK ABOUT IT...

## *Getting It Backward*

Writing in a *Journal for Quality and Participation*, June 1993 (page 84), John Sherwood and Florence Hoylman refer to a *Harvard Business Review* article (Nov.-Dec., 1990) in which Michael Beer explains why most change programs don't result in the changes anticipated:

> "...because they are guided by a theory of change that is fundamentally flawed. The common belief is that the place to begin is with the knowledge and attitudes of individuals. Changes in attitudes...lead to change in individual behavior...And changes in individual behavior, repeated by many people, will result in organizational change...this theory gets the change process exactly backward. In fact, individual behavior is powerfully shaped by the organizational roles that people play. The most effective way to change behavior, therefore, is to put people into a new organizational context, which imposes new roles, responsibilities, and relationships on them."

Of course, reshaping an organization does not in itself bring new life. New wineskins without new wine do not have much value. However, Beer's point is an important one for our church. If we remain in the same environment, retain the same furniture, follow familiar routines, and associate with the same people who repeat the same ideas, we will not get change.

We need a new way of thinking about the church—about what it is and what it does. We need new frameworks, new paradigms, new rules. We need some "mice" to chew on the edges of our institutions, make them inoperable, and force us to rethink and reinvent the congregation for the modern, urban world.

Joel Barker, in *Pioneers* (published by Chart House, Burnsville, Minnesota), a new video about "paradigm pioneers," says change takes:

(1) Intuition

(2) Risk

(3) Time (Don't get in a hurry, or you will merely bring in a new gimmick).

I wish our church systems would be open to new possibilities and would reward people who try and fail as much as they reward those who maintain the status quo and don't foul up. I wish our systems would look at and measure results instead of observing first steps and methods. We could do it, you know. We could lighten up, listen to people on the outside, "unfasten the pews," and open ourselves to new possibilities!

*December 1993*

# A Bishop Responds to Concerns About Quality Improvement

The staff of the General Board of Discipleship have been working for several years to change and improve the way we support the church. We have responded to invitations from the Episcopal leaders of more than half of the conferences in the U.S. and in Puerto Rico to assist with the re-creation of congregational and conference systems. All our efforts continue to focus on the essential work of the church; that is, inviting, forming, and sending.

We began with some fundamental, but simple assumptions:

> *Quality improvement is important in these times...to help us shift our focus as The United Methodist Church from institutional maintenance to a focus on the people and our communities and their needs.*

- The system is designed for the results it is getting.
- If we want different results, we can redesign the system.
- The church's system must be redesigned around people's yearnings for God and the new life that God offers us in Christ.
- To understand people's yearnings, we have to listen to them. The people help their leaders learn how to design good systems.

Sometimes people don't want to change their systems. They may want to improve them, but not to change them. Sometimes people want to change their systems, but they don't want to change the culture, the methods, the language, the vision, or the support processes. Further, in the church, people often want to maintain only those characteristics that—over time—have been designated as sacred.

Some people have objected to our use of business terms and to our use of methods developed for organizations outside the church as we have attempted to design new and appropriate church systems.

The letter that follows is a response by Bishop Sharon Brown Christopher to a letter she received from someone who questioned the appropriateness of the church's borrowing ideas from industry. She responded both as a member of the General Board of Discipleship and as a leader of a conference that is deeply involved in system redesign. She has kindly consented to my sharing her letter.

*June 1994*

*Dear Friend:*

*I write in deep appreciation for the concerns you have shared with me about your perception of the relationship of the Minnesota Annual Conference to Continuous Quality Improvement as it was reflected in a recent **Leader** article. With this letter, I want to respond and to assure you that it is only out of our commitment to God through Jesus Christ that we have been led to incorporate some of the principles of Continuous Quality Improvement into our corporate life as The United Methodist Church in Minnesota. I write not only on my own behalf but also on behalf of the General Board of Discipleship to whom you also addressed your concerns. I am a member of the General Board of Discipleship.*

*I believe that God is doing a radical, new thing among us. Social scientists and theologians tell us that our present time is an evolutionary moment in the life of the western world. They say that 200 years from now, historians will observe that a fundamental shift in the understanding of persons in the western world took place in this evolutionary moment. Social scientists and theologians are calling the times in which we live the "In-between times" because we are living in a time of transition from one age to another.*

*I also believe that we as the church must listen carefully if we are to be faithful to the new thing that God is doing. As one of the leaders of the Minnesota Annual Conference, I intend to invite us as faithful disciples to engage in a careful listening process to God and to one another so that we may discern God's leading and respond to God's will. Our response involves articulating in a new way the vision to which God calls us and the distinct mission that is ours as the church. Our response requires that we examine the United Methodist system that has brought us to this moment and that we improve and redesign—where necessary—that system so that it can be the vehicle that will carry us into the future.*

*I agree that the church is not a business. We do not manufacture products in the way that the business world does. I do not intend—nor does anyone in the Minnesota Annual Conference or the General Board of Discipleship—to make the church a business. Quality improvement is important in these times, I believe, to help us shift our focus as The United Methodist Church from institutional maintenance to a focus on the people and our communities and their needs. It is important to shift the focus of the church's responsibility to the people who live outside the church in our communities and in our world. To help us move in this direction, we have—in fact—been learning from many resources.*

*I root myself firmly in the conviction that God created the world and is active in it. God is not active exclusively in the church. I believe* *that what we celebrate at Christmas is the birth of God in the world, not in the church, and that it was because God so loved the world, not the church, that God sent Jesus to us. I **do not** assume that resources from the world are automatically tainted and are not of God. In fact, I know that Dr. Deming was a faithful disciple in the Episcopal Church. I know that he attended worship regularly, and I suspect that the work in which he was involved for many years was a direct application of his faithfulness.*

*Continuous Quality Improvement as it is practiced in the business world is not applicable directly to the church. The profound knowledge that I know about is the profound knowledge I receive as I grow in my relationship with God. Where Deming's understandings intersect with the life of the church is around the concern of addressing systemic issues that need examination and repair if we are to be faithful to God's leading us into the future. It is at that point that we are appropriating some of Deming's understandings within a theological context.*

*I appreciate greatly the concerns that you raise with me. I hope, through this letter, I am communicating my agreement with you that our focus definitely must be on the activity of God in our midst as it is known in the Christ event. That transcends any secular management tool. It is God's vision alone that we are seeking here in the Minnesota Conference, and we are using the best resources we can to help us align with this task.*

*Sincerely,*

*Sharon A. Brown Christopher*

I don't think I can say it any better than that!

*September 1994*

THINK ABOUT IT...

## Moments of Truth

I spend many nights in hotels each year because of my heavy travel schedule. I have come to notice how much some things matter and how little other things matter. One phone is enough, but I want a clock that I can see in the dark. I don't care if the room is small, but I want a large bed. It is nice to have remote control TV and really hot water in the shower. However, pictures on the wall, mirrors, tables and chairs, and room service are of little concern to me. Most important to me is the ability of the front desk personnel to make me feel that they care more about me than about pleasing the boss.

Although I have encountered significant variation in the quality of hotels, I have found that personal attention and service are what matter most.

Jan Carlson, CEO of Scandinavia Airlines, stressed the importance of personal service when he spoke about "Moments of Truth" with customers in the business world (quoted in *communication briefings*, May 1995). He outlined the following "Moments of Truth" for business:

- How fast and how well the phones are answered.
- The appearance and cleanliness of the business.
- The quality of company stationery.
- The appearance of employees.
- Whether employees smiled and appeared to be pleasant.
- How promptly customers are helped or served.
- How routine customer questions are handled.
- The cleanliness of rest rooms.
- The effectiveness of signs.
- How a product defect or customer complaint is handled.

> *What we measure or focus on should be what matters to people at the deepest levels.*

As I reflected on these, I began to think about possible "Moments of Truth" in congregational life:

- How loving are the people of the congregation?
- How active are church members in building a just world?
- How enthusiastic are members about inviting unchurched people?
- Is there easy access?
- Is there adequate parking?
- Do people have multiple opportunities for worship and participation?
- Do people talk about God and spiritual matters, or do they talk about programs and activities?
- Do the people listen to visitors?
- Do people participate at levels that feel comfortable to them?

- Do people take visitors and new members under their care?
- Do new members have early opportunities to participate in small groups?
- Are individuals' needs addressed?
- Do members have early opportunities to relieve human suffering?

What is important to you in church life? What would you add or take away from the list?

If we listen to people deeply and hear them at deeper levels (deeper perhaps than even they are aware), we might encounter "Moments of Truth" we have never considered.

My friend, Dick Wills, the pastor of Christ Church, Ft. Lauderdale, Florida, pointed out that we tend to focus on what we measure. He has, therefore, been working on a new list of congregational processes to measure. He is addressing the following questions:

(1) Are people's priorities changing—as measured by the stories that they tell? (Dick believes that our priorities don't change unless God is active in our lives.)

(2) Do guests feel welcome?

(3) Are there any "sacred cows"—things that do not contribute to the new priorities?

(4) Are we emphasizing character and spiritual maturity over giftedness and popularity in choosing staff and leadership?

(5) Are members excited about bringing unchurched people to church?

(6) Are new members easily assimilated into the church?

What we measure or focus on should be what matters to people at the deepest levels. To fail to pay significant attention to "Moments of Truth" is to pay attention to lesser matters, to measure the wrong things, and to lose opportunities to reach out to love and serve unchurched people.

*July 1995*

## Always Another Call

In a dialogue published in *Circuit Rider* (June 1995), Bishop Sharon Brown Christopher commented:

> *A core of our tradition as Christians is transformation. Transformation is characterized by the call. God is always calling us and never lets us go, even when we think we have answered the call. There is always another call and another. If we are aligned with God, we are learning, growing persons. It is the activity of the Holy Spirit in our lives.*

As a participant in that dialogue, I appreciated the bishop's powerful statement about the continuing and renewing Christian journey. I later read a tongue-in-cheek "Open Letter" to the Ukrop Brothers by a Virginia Conference Superintendent, Ray Chamberlain, which I also share with you:

> *Dear Ukrop Brothers,*
>
> *Since coming to Richmond I have heard marvelous stories about your stores. I have shopped in them. Eaten in them. Enjoyed them. I have used your mission statement as a model for congregations that are serious about being the church. I have introduced newcomers to your grocery stores and have taken visitors to your Cafe and Grill.*
>
> *But last week I heard one of your employees registering a deep concern about your operation. She understands you are planning to open a new store in Williamsburg and is worried you are getting too big. I also heard someone voice a reservation about the new store you opened on Patterson and Three Chopt, which is only a couple of miles from an old Ukrop store and may attract some of its customers.*
>
> *It's none of my business, but perhaps you might consider scaling back. I mean, just because you have a good thing going and just because people in Williamsburg want you, there is no reason to expand. I guess what I am saying is that you have broken enough new ground—taken enough risks—done enough innovative things—grown large enough. Why not just coast now? Relax.* **Quit visioning!** *Stop reaching out to serve new people. Forget about being on the cutting edge. Leave behind the headaches of finding new markets and new customers. Slow down. Shift into neutral. Slip into reverse!*
>
> *And then one day the Richmond history books will talk about your good old days. About what was. It'll be a mighty fine story.*
>
> *Sincerely,*
>
> *Ray W. Chamberlain, Jr.*
>
> *P.S. By the way, if you need a model for my recommendation, stop by. I can help you. I'm in the business where we have been known to do this sort of thing on a regular basis.*

How many congregations believe that they are "large enough"? How many have "settled in" to defend and continue the status quo?

Wesley would have been appalled—what with all his talk about "being made perfect in love in this life" and "going on to perfection."

Bob Buford (Leadership Network, *Net Fax*, May 15, 1995) has pointed out that we sometimes fail in the church because of our inability to escape the past. At other times, we fail because of our inability to invent the future. Referring to the influential business book *Competing for the Future* by Gary Hamel and C.K. Prahalad (Harvard Business School Press, 1994), Buford summarizes the primary reasons for failure:

### An Inability to Escape the Past

*An Unparalleled Track Record Of Success.* Are you being blinded to the future by your past or present success?

*No Gap Between Expectations and Performance.* Are your expectations exceeding current levels of performance?

*A Contentment with Current Performance.* Are you content with "business as usual" as the norm? "We have always done it this way...why change?"

*An Accumulation of Abundant Resources.* Are you relying on size alone...the accumulation of people (membership), money, and facilities?

*A View That Resources Win Out.* Are membership and budget the only indicators of health that you measure? Are you combining the records of healthy and unhealthy units and obscuring the real situation?

### An Inability to Invent the Future

*An Optimized Business System.* Are you continually examining your structure and staff in light of your mission and an ever-changing environment?

*Deeply Etched Recipes.* Are you relying on the same methods and programs that brought you to today to work in the future?

*A Vulnerability to New Rules.* When the rules change, everyone goes back to zero, and you lose any pervious leverage. Where are you vulnerable if the rules change?

*Success Confirms Strategy.* Are you allowing your present success to determine your future strategy? Are you sacrificing future effectiveness at the expense of today's apparent success?

\* \* \*

Let's hear Bishop Christopher one more time:

*There is always another call and another. If we are aligned with God, we are learning, growing persons. It is the activity of the Holy Spirit in our lives.*

*August 1995*

THINK ABOUT IT...

> "At this moment in The United Methodist Church, we really need **spiritual leaders**...We want spirit-filled companions who are learning daily to walk with Jesus as his disciples and who are inviting us and helping us to learn to walk with Jesus."

# CHAPTER 4:

## MISSION, VISION, AND LEADERSHIP

Leaders with a 100-Year Vision .................................................. 82
Denial .......................................................................................... 84
Who Can Lead Us? ..................................................................... 86
Leadership .................................................................................. 88
Leadership—One More Time ..................................................... 90
Listening to the Laity .................................................................. 92
Ordinary Times ........................................................................... 93
From Conversation to Improvement ......................................... 96
Social Witness ............................................................................ 97
When the Vision Indicts the Present ......................................... 99
"Guranteed Appointment!" I'm For It! ..................................... 102

THINK ABOUT IT...

# Leaders with a 100-Year Vision

*The year is 2091. It is annual conference time. Wesleyan Christians are gathering in more than 150 conference centers around the world to elect delegates to the 2092 session of the General Conference of the World Union of Methodist Churches (formerly The United Methodist Church) in Bangkok, Thailand. The 25-million member Methodist movement now has more congregations in Asia than on any other continent, although Africa and North America each have more members. Bangkok is the center of the church's Asian region. The year 2092 will be the fourth time since 2044 that the General Conference has been held in Southeast Asia.*

*The General Conference of 2092 will have on its agenda issues that have long been important for Methodists—the propagation of the gospel, relief for the poor, hope for the troubled, and world peace. A major attraction at this session will be an all-day drama depicting the denomination's radical transformation during the last century, including:*

- *the globalization of the church;*
- *the reuniting of autonomous Methodist denominations across the world;*
- *the re-emergence of evangelistic zeal, with lay volunteers crisscrossing the globe to engage in partnership initiatives with developing congregations;*
- *the restructuring of annual conferences around long-term visionary strategies for clergy deployment and congregational ministries (beginning with one U.S. Annual Conference in the 1990s).*

*A United Methodist researcher had predicted in 1980 that The United Methodist Church would fold by April 2055 if the membership loss, which had plagued the denomination since 1964, continued at the same rate. However, the latter part of the twentieth century was a time when the church in the U.S. had lost its vision and spirit. Its future was bleak, and there seemed to be no one with the authority to act who could see beyond the present. The church did not dream that one bishop and cabinet in concert with the laity and clergy of one annual conference could restructure the church's ministry and become the renewal spark for a whole denomination.*

Is the above vision merely a pipe dream? I do not think so! We need a vision that stretches into the long-distance future, a vision that will serve as a path out of wandering and loss.

Who will help the church in our day dream of possibilities for the future, based upon values that are and always have been important to Methodists?

### We Need Expanded Visions

The truly great leaders of the world are men and women who have visions of the future that stretch over 100 years. "There is no such thing as leadership per se," says psychologist Elliott Jacques, "but the so-called great leaders through the millennia have a vision of at least 100 years."

Jacques separates outstanding leaders from mediocre ones by assessing how far their visions extend. "The greater your competence, the higher your time horizon," he said, noting that "ordinary mortals" plan only months ahead.

He observed that former Russian leader Gorbachev had a 100-year span of vision and that former Prime Minister Thatcher's vision extends between 50 and 100 years. He believes other world leaders have more limited visions.

A 1991 *Harvard Business Review* article featured a corporation in Japan whose founder and chief executive had a 250-year vision for his company, a vision he communicated and updated each year.

Given such expanded visions, our General Conference emphasis on four-year themes and goals seems limited. Every four years, we wind up the machinery and lay before the church the next four-year emphasis, surrounding it with programs and publicity. Before we can get one emphasis launched, we are busy dreaming up the next one.

What makes great leaders, and where will we find leaders in the church today? Who has the authority and foresight to help the church find a 100-year vision?

While there is no shortage of candidates who are willing to offer a 100-year vision, most who are eager to do so have no way of making any real difference. Only persons with real power and authority can call the church to a vision that stretches 100 years into the future.

One person has joked that since there is no actual head of The United Methodist Church, he will volunteer for the job. That's the crux of the problem: a willing volunteer with no authority to get the job done. Moreover, those who have the power to develop a 100-year vision seem stuck on four-year plans.

We live in a culture that values the quick victory, instant food, quarterly dividends, "one-minute managers," ten-minute oil changes, and the bottom line. We are conditioned for "quick and dirty" solutions. As a result, we have fallen into crisis management, bouncing from one problem to the next.

If 100-year visions are important for world leaders and chief executive officers of corporations, aren't such visions equally important for leaders in the church?

Who in the annual conference will take on the challenge to plan for the life and ministry of congregations over the next 100 years? Who has the hope and courage to step forward and command attention, to set a course that builds toward a new and growing future?

*April 1991*

# Denial

If an organization or system for which I am responsible is not working well, I have two choices:

(1) work to improve it.

(2) deny—
- that it is not working well.
- that it needs fixing (no human institution is perfect).
- that it needs fixing now.
- that it is my responsibility
- that there is anything I can do to fix it, even if it is my responsibility.

> *With so many ways to deny that change is needed and without clarity about who should act, delay in changing or improving a situation could go on forever.*

In July 1988, a new Education Reform Act became law in Great Britain. The National Curriculum Council, was set up to help move the reforms along. Duncan Graham, chief executive of the National Curriculum Council, commented in the May 1991 issue of *The Atlantic* (page 29): "The educational establishment, left to its own, will take a hundred years to buy a new stick of chalk."

I understand that comment. With so many ways to deny that change is needed and without clarity about who should act, delay in changing or improving a situation could go on forever.

*Leadership: A Practical Journal for Church Leaders* (Fall 1990, volume XI, #4) published a story by George Maronge, Jr., who lives in my hometown of Birmingham, Alabama:

> *An old story tells of a desert nomad who awakened hungry in the middle of the night. He lit a candle and began eating dates from a bowl beside his bed. He took a bite from one and saw a worm in it so he threw it out of the tent. He bit into a second date, found another worm, and threw it away also. Reasoning that he wouldn't have any dates left to eat if he continued, he blew out the candle and quickly ate the rest of the dates.*
>
> *Many there are who prefer darkness and denial to the light of reality.*

When an organization is "broken," few argue otherwise. What we argue about is what must be done to fix it and whose responsibility it is.

Suppose the organization in question is The United Methodist Church.

The critical questions are: Who in leadership can no longer deny that the results we are getting in our churches are unacceptable? Is it possible that our connectional system that...

- does not have an executive office at the denominational level,
- has forgotten that the annual conference is the basic system of the church,
- values diversity of viewpoint—about essentials and nonessentials—to the point of divisiveness,
- distributes authority for decision-making to many different people and groups across all levels of the church

...is incapable of repair?

Is that because we are not clear about which leaders have which responsibilities? Denial of responsibility for improvement in The United Methodist Church could go on until the incapacity to act is complete and organizational gridlock precludes action to improve the system.

However, we were not talking about The United Methodist Church. We were talking about schools in faraway Great Britain, about buying chalk, and about denial in general.

I deny that I was talking to or about anybody in particular. So you don't have to take this personally. (But think about it anyway.)

*February 1992*

THINK ABOUT IT...

## Who Can Lead Us?

A number of people responded (many in anger) to my suggestion that the General Council on Ministries, General Council on Finance and Administration, and especially the Council of Bishops can help us work to rebuild and improve some poorly functioning processes and systems in our denomination. Many responded that my solution is "asking the fox to guard the hen house"—that these (and other) general church agencies and leadership groups are the problem.

I both agree and disagree with that sentiment. The aforementioned general church agencies and groups have failed to give leadership at critical junctures. They struggle, as all of us do, to know what to do and how best to do it. Contrary to some beliefs, they are not conspiring to destroy our church.

> *Although we should move away from bureaucratic, top-down management styles, we must receive leadership from those who have the authority to call, inspire, and mobilize the rest of us.*

On the other hand, change—pervasive, appropriate, strategic, long-range transformation of vital United Methodist systems—will not happen spontaneously. Change must be supported by all of us; however, it must be initiated, enforced and reinforced, and led by those we have elected to lead us. Although we should move away from bureaucratic, top-down management styles, we must receive leadership from those who have the authority to call, inspire, and mobilize the rest of us.

Who else could do it?

- One or more of the other general program agencies? No one would suggest this—certainly not I. If you could see the difficulty that we who head the general agencies have working together on a vision and workable processes for moving toward that vision, you would chastise me for even including this suggestion.
- Seminaries? They are on the margins of our denominational system. Increasingly, our pastors are coming from non-United Methodist seminaries, or they are not seminary trained.
- District superintendents? Their authority comes directly from the bishops.
- Pastors? Many are giving able leadership in their congregations or parishes, but even they feel that the connectional system in the annual conference and general church is working against instead of for them. Further, they do not believe they have the authority to do something about the system.

- United Methodist church members? Many members *are* speaking out and *are* doing all they know to do, but they are not mobilized; nor do they have the authority to change things. There is a difference between calling for change and being in a position to put systems in place to bring about the change.

So I come back to the Council of Bishops. The bishops are in a position to get information on primary systems of the denomination, determine improvement strategies, and mobilize the rest of us. They can do it in their own episcopal areas and in the total council for the whole church. Right now, they tend to call on the church to change, but they are not helping us change our systems so that we will get different results.

Perhaps the General Council on Ministries could help the bishops and the rest of us get the information we need to improve our processes. Currently, the council has difficulty getting beyond the trivial and the administration of the status quo.

The General Council on Finance and Administration is the treasurer of the church, and it does that work admirably. This council is in a position to help us rebuild our "out-of sorts" financial system. The General Council on Finance and Administration has the ability:

- to go all the way to the people in the pew, to help hear their longings to give of themselves and their money.
- to facilitate the realization of people's yearnings.
- to reestablish trust between people in ministry and their agents in ministry.
- to offer processes for linking those who give and receive with others in different cultures who give and receive.

So, I stand by my earlier writings on this subject. The Council of Bishops, the General Council on Ministries, and the General Council on Finance and Administration are made up of people elected by the rest of us and accountable to the rest of us. We can blame them, ignore them, or hold them accountable. I'll go with the latter.

*April 1992*

THINK ABOUT IT...

## *Leadership*

> *Consumer criticism spurred by a hostile media crippled the U.S. auto market and obscured progress at General Motors Corp., [former] Chairman Robert Stempel said in a magazine interview.*
>
> *"I haven't seen anything, anywhere—TV, print media—that suggests anything done in the U.S. is good," Stempel told <u>Time</u> magazine in the January 27, 1992, issue...*
>
> *"Certainly the automakers haven't had good press on quality, gas mileage, transmission smoothness."*
>
> *But Stempel acknowledged a turnaround in the media on GM's 1992 Cadillac Seville, which won several automotive press awards.*
>
> *"I am pleased at the reaction on the new Seville," he said. "Finally we've seen some breakthrough."*
>
> (From *The Tennessean,* January 20, 1992)

No wonder General Motors is in trouble. Couldn't former Chairman Stempel see that...

- It doesn't matter what the press says because people will buy what has quality;
- General Motors built a better automobile—the Cadillac Seville—and people are buying it;
- Blaming consumers rather than listening to them is General Motors' problem.

We know that...

- If General Motors makes quality automobiles, the automobiles will sell.
- If General Motors offers good value (quality related to price), people will flock to the showrooms.
- If General Motors listens to people who buy cars (not just to those who bought General Motors cars in the past), the company will know how to build quality automobiles and give customers good value.
- If General Motors gets good leadership at the top (top managers taking responsibility for quality), General Motors can delight its customers and increase its competitive share of the automobile market.
- General Motors needs leadership appropriate to the automobile business; that is, someone who knows quality in automobiles, how to build them, and how to sell them.

I worry about the leadership at the top of several large U.S.-based companies: General Motors, IBM, Sears, American Express, and others. I worry because what they do affects you and me. I worry, too, because the leaders of church organizations who "grew up" with these companies are not doing very well either. (That includes me.)

In Mr. Stempel's defense, I believe he was set up to fail. He was given leadership in a system that was entrenched in nineteenth century management methods—as is the church—and although he began change, it was so late coming that the change could not satisfy stockholders and directors. His biggest mistake was to report monumental losses while he was at the helm.

Leaders in The United Methodist Church, for the most part, are not given organizational systems that are capable of improvement. Those of us placed in leadership positions don't know that when we take on our new positions. We overestimate our abilities. We correctly assume that improvement is possible, but we usually have little clue about how to institute improvement. We keep trying until we find something that works.

However, little works because the system is not capable of long-term improvement without basic change. That takes leadership, and most of us know only how to manage.

The solution is to be honest about our system. We can train and retrain our present leaders to lead. We can help them get leadership knowledge and perspective on systems change. We can also help leaders of the future understand the kind of skills that will be needed for the future and assist them to choose appropriately where they will serve.

Three days before the above *Tennessean* story ran, *Newscope* ( a weekly United Methodist newsletter) carried the following lines: "Maxie Dunnam, evangelist and senior pastor of Christ UMC in Memphis, Tennessee, has declined an invitation from the Memphis Conference delegation to become a candidate for the episcopacy. 'To be an effective bishop, one must be called. . . I honestly do not feel that call at this time,' he said."

For me, that is leadership—leadership appropriate to the church. I don't know how to explain it, but I would prefer that the bishop of my annual conference be someone who is called rather than someone who has run a successful political race. The present state of our church may support my case.

A few days after that item appeared in *Newscope*, another front-running episcopal candidate in a different region told me about Maxie's action and said that he was strongly considering taking the same stand. He did. Both he and Maxie were likely winners, in my judgment, if they had stayed in the race. However, they both saw the rigidity of the present system and opted to stay in their present roles.

Is it possible that one or two persons could change the way we now get our leaders—merely by withdrawing? Is it possible we could reappraise our present systems and be more honest with candidates for leadership (at all levels) about the radical change that is needed, expected, and that we will support? If we don't, our church will get weaker. As it becomes more precarious and more difficult to survive, our leaders will opt more readily for short-term posturing, and their vision will be to keep the ship afloat until the next sentry's watch.

*April 1993*

## Leadership – One More Time

An organization needs leaders who are appropriate to the organization's mission and circumstances. However, leaders are set up to fail when:

- They are given organizations that are incapable of improvement.
- They do not understand the depth of change needed.
- They overestimate their ability to lead change.
- They are not given time or authority to redesign the organizational system.
- They know only how to manage.

The church—as any institution—needs a system that clearly defines for its leaders the kind of leadership the system needs. Some leaders are able to see the kind of change that is needed and can decide whether or not they can provide such change. Many of us, however, do not see the real leadership task until we are in a leadership position; and then it may be too late.

Earlier, I talked about leadership at General Motors and in the church, and I pointed to the necessity of having leadership appropriate to the organization at a given time and place. Upon more reflection, I realize I may have given the impression that it is better to reject leadership in The United Methodist Church today than to seek leadership. I do not believe that. Because they felt the call of God to seek leadership as pastors, lay leaders, bishops, general secretaries, or holders of other positions in the church, hundreds of United Methodist leaders today *are the right people in the right places* to help our church be more responsible to the people we have the opportunity to serve. I am grateful for the leadership of these people. As never before, leaders are demonstrating a desire (a passion even) to change systems, to change paradigms, and to change their own approaches to leadership to produce different results.

However, I still see two major areas of concern:

(1) Some people who see that the present system is impenetrable are choosing not to accept leadership. They choose to remain where they know they can function effectively. I applaud that! However, we *are* losing some of our best talent. I am truly concerned about the young men and women in our congregations who choose not to enter the pastoral leadership of our church because they see the church as dysfunctional.

(2) Some of us who have accepted or sought roles of responsibility realize the limitations of the present system only when we are in those roles. Some of us are not aware early enough that leading—not managing existing structures—is required. Some of us do not see that leading and managing a system are different.

Part of the problem is that our societal paradigm teaches us that good leaders can work miracles. We've seen the wonders worked by John Kennedy, Martin Luther King, Jr., John Wesley, and others. However, most of us are not in that category of leaders, and most of us cannot or will not lead at that level.

## CHAPTER 4: MISSION, VISION, AND LEADERSHIP

Further, scores of factors beyond leadership influence outcomes.

Another reality in The United Methodist Church today is that the system of boundaries, limitations, checks, and balances that we put into place over the years now presents a barrier for changing the system. It seems that no single intervention into the system to change it can overcome the inertia or penetrate deeply enough to alter its basic character. Moreover, we seem incapable of attempting more than one intervention at a time. Too many of us are holding on to what we think is important and feel we can't risk losing what is left. Further, some of us want the *position* of leadership more than we want to lead. We are more interested in status than in the results of ministry.

If more of us understood that the systems we are called upon to lead are incapable of or are highly resistant to improvement under the present rules, we would think twice about taking those jobs.

If our systems were more hospitable to strong leadership, while at the same time rejecting top-down or autocratic leadership, we who are in positions of responsibility would have a better chance of facilitating change.

How many of our leaders today have assumed roles they could not possibly fill well, but they did not know it? They have tried and have reaped frustration.

My primary concerns, then, about leadership in The United Methodist Church are:

(1) Many of the best and brightest of our people will not choose leadership in a system that appears incapable of improvement and that does not support and reward good leadership.

(2) We must not continue to put people in leadership positions for which they are not adequately prepared—either because they do not understand the nature or the extent of the leadership required, or because they do not have adequate knowledge for the task.

Ordaining a pastor or consecrating a diaconal minister or a bishop does not make those persons leaders. A layperson who has agreed to take leadership in the congregation may not be equipped for the task.

Usually, we assume that there are three steps to leadership—recruiting, training, and deploying. I believe that in our church—at every level—another step is necessary: Those recruited and trained for leadership need an adequate understanding of the change and type of leadership needed *before they are deployed as leaders.*

Is our present system capable of providing our leaders with this kind of clarity and perspective?

*July 1993*

THINK ABOUT IT...

## Listening to the Laity

Julian Dyke, president of the Polycystic Kidney Research Foundation, former Boy Scout executive, and a man known by thousands as a person who lives and shares his faith every day in every way he can, wrote recently to Episcopalian Bishop Ronald Haines at the National Cathedral in Washington, D.C. Dyke also sent me a copy. One paragraph in the July 22 [1993] letter was striking to me in its simplicity. He went to the heart of the need of both laity and clergy in the church today:

> *"As we look at the ministry of the people of God in and beyond the boundaries of the gathered church, it is important to remind ourselves that lay persons look to the church for guidance and for experiences where they can be renewed and sustained in their ministry. Clergy need help in their roles of teaching and counseling lay ministers."*

If we could help our clergy perform their roles, the clergy could help our laity fulfill their ministry.

In a July 1993 letter, Lem Tanksley, a mechanical engineer and a long-time member of Belle Meade United Methodist Church in Nashville, wrote:

> *"Leadership is the church's greatest challenge. The time is NOW. Leadership is EVERYTHING. I am putting down my thoughts, gleaned over the years in business. What is this mysterious force called "leadership"? It is true that great leaders can be extroverts or introverts, exuberant or reserved, articulate or inarticulate. Leaders do not come from some wondrous leadership mold designed in the sometimes barren waste of Academia. But the qualities of leaders need not be a mystery.*
>
> *"First, they must love the church. The best leaders love what they do; their work is in their blood. They have deep feelings about operating the church well, about helping it grow. The combination of natural enthusiasm and doing what one loves to do produces the emotional energy of leadership. The leader's love of the church is contagious, and others learn to love the church, too. The leader's calling becomes the calling of many.*
>
> *"Second, all great leaders have a vision. Leaders believe in their vision (which is as much values as strategy) and are rarely distracted from it. Their persistence and their constancy of theme and action give the vision wings. Leaders who do not believe in something can't be leaders. Leaders are students of change. They view continuous innovation as the life blood. They seek change to deliver the vision. Leaders seek the new to strengthen the old.*
>
> *"Third, leaders are workers. They not only have a vision, they work unusually hard to execute it well. Leaders are implementers, not just strategists; doers, not just dreamers. Leaders are obsessed with doing things right. They continually sound the trumpet of excellence. They have high expectations for themselves and for everyone else they influence. They fundamentally believe in the capacity of people to achieve. I believe that the best leaders are actually the 'Servant Leaders' who stay off the pedestal and use the powers of office to help people succeed."*

No comment. I can't improve on that.

*November 1993*

CHAPTER 4: MISSION, VISION, AND LEADERSHIP

## *Ordinary Times*

Bishop H. Hasbrouck Hughes led the Florida Conference Cabinet in worship on the last day of a "Quest for Quality" seminar. For three days, participants had talked about who we are as the church of Jesus Christ, our vision for the future, how we can replace a system that has grown tired with one that will empower us to be the church in the present age, and the nature of leadership that can facilitate the transition to a different future.

In reflecting on leadership, Bishop Hughes quoted the historian Henry Adams regarding the leadership of Louis XVIII of France:

> "He would have done well in ordinary times. Unfortunately he inherited a revolution and was unable to stem the tide."

### We Inherited a Revolution

Those of us in leadership positions in the church inherited a revolution too, although we may not have recognized it. Whether we became leaders in mid-century or in recent times, we assumed that our denomination had merely lost its way and that we could help it find its way.

> *We have been thrust into a revolution in all parts of our lives, and the church is no longer a place of refuge. The problem is that the church must be a place where people can cling to that which is enduring in the midst of the chaos.*

Most of us in the ordained and consecrated ministry attended orthodox seminaries and were schooled in the classical tradition. We learned—and most of us learned well—the story of our Christian past and how the great thinkers of the church helped us clarify the essential and enduring belief structure upon which we have built global institutions.

However, we didn't know that we were signing on to lead a revolution. That's a large part of our current problem: We did not agree to lead a revolution. We are not prepared, and we don't want to do it. Most of us don't like revolutions, controversy, or chaos. We seek order, stability, and *gradual* improvement.

Most of us would have probably done well in *ordinary times*. During the period that preceded the industrial revolution (and to some degree during the building of industrialized societies), there were long stretches of stability in communities and in the institutions that served them. We had plenty of good leaders for that period. Perhaps we were just born too late!

Our institutions—including the church—were constructed to operate in those earlier, *ordinary times*—times of stability and gradual growth. The

United Methodist Church—in its understanding of mission, its outlook for the future, its structure and processes, and its organizational system—was designed for ordinary times—times marked by slow change, defined community orientation, and homogenous lifestyles and congregations. As a result, our multi-million member church is organized to do everything by old, fixed rules in a world that demands change and customization. *We can't deal with it.*

We are a denomination that trusts the recruitment and training of its precinct leaders to chance and to the whim of those who present themselves. We are committed to freedom of choice (or perhaps to a philosophy of *laissez faire*), so *we can't deal with it.*

We talk about the need to take seriously the ministry of the laity, ministry with the poor and marginal, the extension of the church in new communities in far-flung places, and openness to all people. However, *we can't deal with it.* Our denomination was designed and engineered for *ordinary times*—friendly times, times of sameness and symmetry. We are designed for *no change*—and we're getting it.

We don't have to sacrifice our church on the altar of relativity, or gimmickry, or fad. We don't have to move precipitously or with lack of clarity about our direction. However, we do have to act soon to change.

Many of our laity, pastors, conference leaders, and general church leaders are expressing frustration—and sometimes anger—about the current state of the church. However, some who have achieved status in the old system want to preserve the status quo. Others have given up on the possibility of change.

There is little satisfaction for any of us today. We have been thrust into a revolution in all parts of our lives, and the church is no longer a place of refuge. The problem is that the church *must* be a place where people can cling to that which is enduring in the midst of the chaos. But for the church to be that place, its leaders must live through the revolution with the people.

Those of us in leadership didn't ask for, want, or prepare for living through a revolution. We are frustrated, anxious, and nervous. We are afraid that the system will implode, and that we will be held responsible. (And we should be.)

A system is vulnerable when it is:

- incapable of stopping activity.
- designed to keep adding activities until something works.
- attaining higher and higher thresholds of frustration and dissatisfaction.
- experiencing increasing rule and boundary violations.
- measuring its results by the level of giving to maintain causes and structures that are poorly understood.
- inept at and unexcited about listening to the people it serves and can serve.
- blaming its workers for system defects.
- blaming its beneficiaries for not benefiting.

Those of us with the title "leader" (person in charge) are likely to be held responsible—at least in the courts of pubic opinion—for the system's vulnerability. However, this is not the time for blame or fault-finding. It is the time for us to act differently. The chaos of a revolution is upon us. We have options: We can put on our armor and wade into the fray, swinging wildly. We can back off, retrain for the task at hand, and take responsibility as learning leaders. We can move aside and invite those who can lead in revolutions to take our places.

### What if...

...someone sent in a petition to the next General Conference that read, "Other legislation not withstanding, each annual conference has the authority to organize appropriately for ministry in its area." (And what if it passed?)

...in the next Episcopal elections that follow General Conference, we elected more leaders who are comfortable leading a revolution?

...we worked harder to identify the laity who could help lead a revolution? What if we prayed with them and invited them to consider ordained or consecrated leadership in the church?

...we worked harder to identify the laity who could lead a revolution? And what if we "leaders" fell in line behind them?

What if...?

*March 1994*

## From Conversation to Improvement

A 1994 issue of *Viewpoint*, a publication of the General Council on Ministries, summarized the results of an Issues Forum held in January on "Spiritual Leadership Into the 21st Century." The article, written by David Severe, states that there are three "prominent implications": lay empowerment, clergy excellence, and global scope and vision.

Who would argue about the significance of these three issues?

Severe, in his conclusion, states:

> *Who can help us change or improve our system so that we can...put spiritual leaders in our congregations and empower our laity for faith development and discipleship to the ends of the earth?*

"The General Council on Ministries is not expected to propose legislation as a result of this event. Our hope is that the ideas generated at the Issues Forum will resurface amidst the work of groups and agencies across the church as they struggle with their own mission statements and their specific mandates. In that sense, we may never know what new direction was a direct result of this event's dialogue. That is not important. What is important is that we continue to find ways for conversation to be held around issues which affect all of our lives and the future of our church."

My question is, who can take action on these issues? Who can help us change or improve our system so that we can act on these issues to put spiritual leaders in our congregations and empower our laity for faith development and discipleship to the ends of the earth? Who can help us create a church that can move from conversation to improvement?

Who?

I think it is really important for us to answer these questions.

*July 1994*

## Social Witness

In *The Christian Century* (April 28, 1993, p. 446), Donald Lindskoog summarizes his view of various denominations with one word or two-word phrases to describe the special gifts each brings to the whole church:
Baptists—*evangelism*
Lutherans and Episcopalians—*worship*
Presbyterians and Reformed—*theological thoroughness*
United Church of Christ and United Methodists—*social witness*

His summary does not surprise me. I have long known that people outside our denomination think of Methodists historically as being active in social concerns.

As a person engaged in the work of the General Board of Discipleship, I might wish another term best described our denomination (such as discipleship, evangelism, zeal, spirituality, or lay ministry); but I don't. I would not have it any other way. One of the ends of our efforts in the church is to affirm that the whole world—and each of us—is God's. God created the world; God is redeeming it; and we are God's stewards. We are faithful disciples when we follow Jesus *into the world*. In the church, we receive people and relate them to God. The Christian community nurtures people and sends them out to live socially conscious lives. That is who Methodists have been historically and who we want to be today and in the future.

> *The Christian community nurtures people and sends them out to live socially conscious lives.*

I have come to believe that it is more important for United Methodist leaders to help congregations develop socially sensitive and responsible Christians than it is for the leaders to tell the world what they think about specific issues (as if what leaders think is better or more important and as if making statements is more important than taking action). When people hear a leader state his or her view, they may disagree with that particular leader's stand and, therefore, do not examine the issue more closely and make unbiased decisions.

People today increasingly care about the larger society, and we all need help in understanding the issues and implications of various actions. When church leaders tell people what to do, the people either cease to think about the issues and accept a handed down "truth"; or—more likely—they ignore the leaders and consider the issues apart from the Christian community.

Martin Marty, in the May 9-16, 1993, issue of *The Christian Century* (p. 583) talks about how he and William Sloan Coffin were criticized by John Frohnmayer, former chairman of the National Endowment for the Arts, for not speaking in defense of the NEA when it was attacked on the issue of artistic freedom. After reading that article, I began to ponder anew how people outside the church may be looking to leaders of the church—people placed in

# Think About It...

high positions by the church—to speak *for the church* in the face of injustice. Not all people in the church have the authority or the means to speak and be heard as do certain leaders.

But then my ministry of the laity bias arose, and I found myself wondering why all sorts of people, who happen also to be church people, could not speak out in behalf of (or against) artistic freedom or whatever issue. Could they not address the issues as well as those persons we have placed in leadership positions? It is true that many who speak out would not be recognized as representing the church. However, as more people spoke out in the context of their faith in God and in the pursuit of justice and caring in the world, they would be recognized; and the dialogue would be joined on more fronts. Further, what is important is not that people speak in the name of their religious faith or their denomination, but that they have knowledge and that they speak with conviction as they address the basic issues facing humankind. All of us are stewards of God in all the world and all the people belong to all of us. We must take responsibility.

It has always interested me that the United Methodist General Board of Church and Society constantly has to state that it does not speak for the denomination. Since that is the case, why have representatives of that agency speak to people outside the church at all? Why not have that board present all sides of important issues to those of us *inside the church* so that we can intelligently discuss the issues and act in ways that will make a difference?

I wish it were possible for all United Methodists to speak and act as a part of (and in behalf of) the Christian community. I wish it were possible for my church to help me reflect on the complex issues of poverty, injustice, racism, and the sanctity of human life. I wish my church could help me see all sides of the issues, including why people differ so radically on the difficult issues.

I don't need to be told what to think. But I do need some help understanding all the implications.

*December 1994*

CHAPTER 4: MISSION, VISION, AND LEADERSHIP

# When the Vision Indicts the Present

A delicate and sometimes confusing relationship exists between current reality and future possibilities. I have been analyzing this relationship with scores of groups these past five years. Occasionally, the desired vision is merely an improved version of the present situation. However, people most often want a very different future—a house that cannot be built with the bricks of the present dwelling.

The problem comes when people are ready to move from the old to the new. Their experience of more "normal" times (in the past) has been that change comes gradually. They, therefore, want to believe that as long as they change in the "right direction," they are moving toward a new and better way. But if the change involves leaping a chasm between "the way it is" and "the way it can be," incremental change is inadequate.

A friend of mind keeps bees as a hobby. He told me that if you want to move a hive of bees from one part of the yard to another, you must initially move them at least a mile away for a few weeks. Later, you can move them to their new home. Otherwise, the bees would return to the original location of their hives, and they would eventually die.

Sometimes when we want to make even a small change in the church, we have to create a new setting for the change that is far enough removed from the old setting that we can develop new patterns and processes. But creating a new setting seems unnecessary much of the time. We can't see that the change we are seeking may be of an entirely different character.

We find it hard to believe that "when a paradigm shifts, everything goes back to zero" (Joel Barker). We don't understand that our past experiences and learnings may not be valid and that we may have to begin anew to relearn even the basics. For example, people who are learning to use computers must develop a whole new set of skills, thought patterns, and ways of working. In the church setting, consider how people who associate silence and stillness with seeking and waiting for God might react to applause during worship services and laughter and talking at gathering times before worship. We don't move to new paradigms by incrementally changing the old paradigm.

We have been making significant changes at the General Board of Discipleship. We have attempted to change the way we think as we have shifted from focusing on products and services to focusing on people. We are moving from bureaucratic hierarchy to team work and from perfecting the parts to perfecting the whole. We have made great improvements in many ways. We are learning more every day. Unfortunately, we have not yet changed our fundamental paradigm—our basic assumption—our primary story. Until we do, we will not be in a position to support and resource The United Methodist Church as it faces the radical discontinuities between the modern and post-modern world. If we don't make the paradigm change, we will continue getting essentially the same results.

Two recent conversations helped me to see both how far we have come (in the old paradigm) and how far we have to go to change our paradigm (and possibly get far different results).

In one conversation, a staff member of the General Board of Discipleship expressed shock when I said that I had great expectations for staff participation in decision-making (in areas such as work assignments and salary negotiations) when the board finally has self-directed, shared leadership work teams. My colleague expressed the belief that the improved patterns of working together had already brought staff within her unit to true team status.

After reflecting on our differing perspectives, I realized that my colleague had interpreted my different vision (a radically different one) as a negative evaluation of the present. Further, my colleague could not see that my vision for the future is predicated on different assumptions from those of the present. The present state—even in its most improved form—cannot deliver the new vision. The conversation was frustrating for both of us. My colleague was frustrated that our extensive improvement is not enough. I was frustrated by my inability to bring about the fundamental change in assumptions that will make our new vision possible.

That same week, I had a conversation with a woman who was participating (with 150 others) in a seminar I was leading on change. I believed that the whole group had agreed that the *status quo* could no longer be tolerated, but this woman asked me later why we needed to improve. She said, "The United Methodist Church attracted me and all the people in this room. If it is meeting our needs, why won't it do the same for others? Don't you believe that God is already present in our church? How can we improve on that?" Well, I can't improve on that.

Hers were tough questions, and the answers are not simple ones. I later realized that she and I were working from different assumptions. Hers was, "If it's working—or working for some—don't tamper with it!" Mine was (and is), "If it can be better, let's improve it!" I think underlying her words was also a belief that the "knowns" of the present (albeit imperfect) system are preferable to the "unknowns" of a different system.

Her remarks and those of my colleague helped me understand what many people have been telling me:

(1) Just because there is a lot of frustration with the system doesn't mean that everyone is seeking change.

(2) The present is more comfortable than the unknown future.

(3) It is one thing to understand paradigm change in theory; it is another to understand how paradigm change differs from a *trend* that brings incremental change.

(4) We don't know how to change paradigms. We *may* know how to manage present processes.

(5) Current reality may be acceptable to people who have never known anything better. For those who have envisioned a different future, however, present reality may be intolerable.

(6) The statement of a new vision—particularly one that can be attained only through a different kind of system—may be interpreted by people who have tried to make the old system work as an indictment of their efforts and an unfair criticism.

Pastors and members of conference cabinets tell me that they often experience this same phenomenon. We must find a way to deal with it.

Perhaps one response is that a new vision must always be clearly differentiated from current reality. Leaders must make sure that they (1) listen carefully and state current reality honestly; and (2) state the new vision (which must be shared and confirmed by the people) *in a way that clearly reveals the gap between reality and the future.*

Pastors who entered the United Methodist ministry in the last third of the twentieth century may never have known the church to work connectionally. Therefore, they may see nothing amiss in the rapid move to congregationalism. They wonder, "Why rebuild a covenanted ministry with shared ownership by all?"

Some staff of the General Board of Discipleship joined our agency, hoping to pursue their specific professional interests. (And their expertise in particular areas was probably why we hired them.) Most of the staff had never thought about subsuming their career interests to the re-creation of the denomination—which is the task before us now.

The boards and agencies of our church in congregations, conferences, and the general church have always essentially had autonomy. The Council on Ministries' coordinating role hasn't altered the autonomy of those bodies much. The various agencies pursue their own work. We are all friendly with one another, but we don't work out of the same vision and assumptions.

I have made assumptions that most leaders want the extensive change that I want, that current reality is intolerable, that we can learn a better way, that our short-term system can be made to function long-term.

I have come to realize, however, that some want less change than I. Some want more. Change is harder than I thought. It would help me to know what you…think about it.

*May 1995*

THINK ABOUT IT...

# "Guaranteed Appointment!" I'm For It!

*The United Methodist annual conference, led by the bishop and cabinet and other conference leaders, will guarantee every congregation, mission, special ministry and all the people who worship, serve, or participate in United Methodist faith communities a **spiritual leader** every time a new leader is appointed or deployed.*

That's what I want and what I believe we all want: *the guaranteed appointment of a **spiritual leader**.*

We want other things too, but nothing is as important or as fundamental to everything else as having spiritual leaders to pray for us and with us in our faith communities. In the church, we want to serve and to be served. We want to experience fellowship and caring community with others. We want to nurture and to be nurtured, to teach and to learn with others. We want to give and to receive.

In the church, we want to learn God's word—from the Bible and from the testimony of Augustine, Aquinas, Luther, Wesley, Albright, Otterbein, Hoosier, Theresa, and all the saints through the centuries. We want to hear God's word in our day as God speaks to us and through our leaders and neighbors.

United Methodists—both the present and the future ones—want to learn to pray, to participate in the sacraments and the ordinances of the church, and to celebrate God's love in public worship.

We United Methodists want to experience our faith in the church so that we can live our faith in the world. We want to rehearse it in the faith community so we can practice it faithfully when we are away from the gathered church. We want to be agents of love, mercy, grace, and compassion wherever we go. We want to live and learn and act with justice, righteousness, and truth.

At this moment in The United Methodist Church, we really need *spiritual leaders*. Confident that together we can work out the rest of it, we want pastors, teachers, administrators, and supervisors who can lead us to God. We want spirit-filled companions who are learning daily to walk with Jesus as his disciples and who are inviting us and helping us to learn to walk with Jesus. We want people who have been sent by the church into leadership ministries because they have personally experienced the power of God's transformation in their own lives. We want leaders who have learned and are *still learning* how to facilitate that transformation for others. We want leaders who are wise in things of the spirit and of the world. We want leaders who can help us seek where God is moving and working and who can encourage us to be part of it.

We do not mean to imply that we want leaders too perfect to exist in the real world. Not at all! We simply want as leaders women and men who are themselves being transformed by God and who know enough about leading others to invite us on the journey.

Conference leaders, if you will give us spiritual leaders, we *will* work the rest of it out together.

Is such leadership too much to ask of The United Methodist Church today? Is it too much to ask of our church five years from now — or ten

## CHAPTER 4: MISSION, VISION, AND LEADERSHIP

years? Is it too much to ask that we begin today to move toward it? Conference leaders, can you deliver what we most want?

Of course, you can! We know you can, because we have experienced such leadership on occasion. We therefore know that such leadership is possible. We also believe that you want what we want. For a few years, would you consider leaving everything else aside to help us improve our systems to get a few more spiritual leaders next year than this year? If you did that, in ten years we would be a very different church. We are not asking you to do it alone. We are asking you to help us.

It doesn't matter to us whether the leaders you send us are ordained, consecrated, or lay. They may be of any age, race, or gender. Further, we are disgusted with the classism, ageism, racism, and sexism that invade our systems when we do not have leaders who keep us focused on Christ.

Not only do we want our pastors to be spiritual leaders, but we also want our Sunday school teachers, class leaders, small group leaders, and all who carry responsibility for programs and committees in the church to be spiritual leaders. We want to be spiritual leaders ourselves. We can work on developing spiritual leaders in our congregations — *if* you will send us spiritual leaders to be our pastors.

Is it too much to ask that the church be about the task of spiritual formation and transformation and that we have leaders who can lead that transformation? If we are willing to give up our requests for creative programmers, trained managers, and experienced problem solvers, is it too much to ask that we get a pastor who will listen to us, pray with us, and hold our vision on high?

Our conference leaders need to hear us say how it feels when we don't have spiritual leaders as pastors. We feel abandoned. We feel we have been abandoned by our church; some of us may even feel abandoned by God. It hurts! It hurts deeply!

It does not just hurt on Sunday morning. The feeling of abandonment affects who we are and what we do. It affects our lives and those around us in countless ways.

Our responses to the feelings of abandonment vary. Some of us flee — drop out or go elsewhere. Some of us fight — we get angry and defensive and ornery. Most of us just don't understand. We think our feelings of abandonment are our fault, and we don't know what to do.

We do not want to cast blame. We understand that our present denominational system cannot deliver consistently the one thing our congregations most need—pastors seeking pure hearts before God. But we believe our present system can be redesigned, and we want our leaders to know that we want that more than anything.

When I served as a pastor, I was not the spiritual leader that I am now asking my pastor to be. I am sorry for that. In those days, I thought it was more important to get it right (theologically) and do it right (methodologically) than to image Christ in my life and work. I remember that as a pastor I had a deep desire to be a spiritual leader, but I felt keenly my inability and my lack of support.

I believe that pastors today want to be spiritual leaders. To help them, we will have to subordinate everything else we are doing and put a system in place that will produce spiritual leaders. We will then have a base in our church for both being and doing everything else we want as a United Methodist Church. We will have the capability of ridding our church of the division, barriers, and sins that plague us.

"Guaranteed Appointment!" I'm for it! A *spiritual leader* every time in every place is our plea.

*P.S. - To Conference Leaders—*

If you hear us and love us, but you cannot deliver us a spiritual leader this time, we beg you to do one of two things:

(1) Don't send us a leader at all. We are people of faith, and we can be spiritual companions for one another until we can call out one or a team from our church to lead us, or until you can send us a spiritual leader.

*or*

(2) Send us a pastor who wants to be a spiritual leader and who is willing to learn. We will lead, love, and "learn" him or her into leadership. But please be honest with us and tell us what you are doing so we won't expect one thing and get another.

*December 1995*